OTHER BOOKS BY THIS AUTHOR:

The Doctors Guide to Starting Your Practice/Career Right

The Doctors Guide to Eliminating Debt

The Doctors Guide to Smart Career Alternatives and Retirement

The Doctors Guide to Navigating a Financial Crisis

THE DOCTORS

GUIDE TO

Real Estate Investing for Busy Professionals

(Who Don't Think Real Estate Is for Them)

DR. CORY S. FAWCETT

The Doctors Guide to Real Estate Investing for Busy Professionals
(Who Don't Think Real Estate Is for Them)
By Dr. Cory S. Fawcett © 2019

Print ISBN: 978-1-61206-189-4
eBook ISBN: 978-1-61206-190-0

Interior and Cover Design by: Fusion Creative Works, FusionCW.com
Lead Editor: Jennifer Regner

For more information, visit FinancialSuccessMD.com

To purchase this book at discounted prices, go to AlohaPublishing.com or email alohapublishing@gmail.com

Published by

AlohaPublishing.com
Printed in the United States of America

Dedication

I dedicate this book to the memory of my grandparents, Orshal and Virginia Brown. They showed me the value of investment real estate to one's financial future and that anyone can become a real estate investor.

Dr. Cory S. Fawcett

Contents

Twelve years after purchasing my first apartment complex (followed by four more), my real estate investments were producing more passive income than I was spending, which enabled me to retire from general surgery at age 54. I want to show you why real estate investing can be better than even your 401(k) for creating retirement income—maybe better than many other types of investments—and how I did it, because there's a lot of misinformation floating around about real estate investing.

When I'm talking about owning a real estate investment, I mean purchasing actual rental income-producing property. Not a REIT (real estate investment trust), not crowdfunding, not syndication. This type of investment has several great benefits, including cash flow (which I now live on), appreciation (which your kids will inherit), the ability to leverage the purchase (massive profits), and—my favorites—depreciation (we all crave fewer taxes), and the flexibility to spend those profits when and how we choose (freedom).

A real estate investor evaluates and purchases property with cash flow and profit as bottom-line requirements. The reluctant landlord is someone who got stuck with something they never intended to rent out and tried to make it work. The outcome of these two methods of acquiring real estate is predictable. The difference is in choosing and evaluating properties for your intended purpose. I'll show you how to identify a reluctant landlord so you can avoid taking advice from people who don't know how to be a successful real estate investor.

I'll walk you through my very first purchase, a 31 unit apartment complex I bought for over a million dollars with no money down. This is not a hypothetical example of what could happen, but a real deal, something not seen much in real estate books. Most people don't understand what a no-money-down real estate transaction really means, and there's plenty of misinformation about this, including the thought that you can't do it anymore. I hope that by showing you what I did, it will make your first purchase a lot less scary and you will realize that you can do it too.

Real estate investing is buying for the long term, and it must produce cash flow in the first year. If it can't produce cash flow from the beginning, don't buy it. So there's no need to wait for lower prices, and it's usually easier to buy when the market is not "hot." What you are looking for is a win-win deal—not distressed properties or a great bargain that you can flip. Save those deals for people with a lot of time on their hands. You're too busy for that.

Understand what you're looking for and how, as a busy professional, you can find what you want without wasting time making multiple offers that get turned down. Part of this is deciding exactly what kinds of properties you want to buy and how to find them. I'll explain the pros and cons of some of the different types of investment properties so you can start with your favorite.

There's a difference between screening a potential property for purchase and evaluating its true profit potential—and you need to use different methods for each. I'll explain the nuts and bolts and some terms so you understand how to screen properties and educate your real estate agent on how to do it too. To save yourself significant time, your agent needs to know how to recognize the "plums."

If there's any magic in this book, this is it. Screening properties narrows your options, but you have to collect more information about the property to evaluate its cash flow potential before making an offer. It also determines the price you are willing to pay and makes the decisions simple: if you can't get it for the price and terms you need for positive cash flow, walk away. You can't rely on a real estate agent's advice for this. It's the most important part of buying real estate investment property and you must do this yourself.

Chapter 8: How to Finance Real Estate Investment Property   141

How you finance a real estate investment property is a critical part of the equation. I'll show you some of the ways it can be done, and surprisingly few of them involve a bank. When you understand the source of risk in these transactions, everything becomes simpler. I'll show you how I did it and dispel some myths about the process.

Chapter 9: Making the Offer   167

Once you've evaluated the property for cash flow and financing options, you're ready to make an offer. I always look for win-win deals—a win for both the buyer and the seller. You're not making multiple offers—there won't be many properties that meet your criteria for a good investment, plus you don't have the time for that. Making good offers on only the right properties saves you both time and money.

Chapter 10: Tips and Tricks to Managing Real Estate   185
          for Busy Professionals

My wife and I did every aspect of managing and working on the apartment the first year we owned it. We wanted to know what it took to properly care for a property. The next year, we delegated the parts we didn't want to do and became the manager, which took about 10-15 hours a month at our peak of 64 units. After I retired from medicine and started traveling, we turned all the management over to a property management company to make our investment totally passive. You can choose what you want to do and hire out the rest—or all of it. I'll show you what we learned about the process, which is valuable to know whether you do it yourself or pay someone else.

Chapter 11: The Pros and Cons of Property   219
          Management Companies

You can still have positive cash flow on an investment property, even if you don't do any of the management. Understand what management companies do and how they do it, so you can make the decision that's right for you—and so you know if they are doing it correctly.

Have an income target in mind when you begin investing, or you won't know when to stop. Over seven years, we purchased five apartment complexes. I probably would have kept on buying but after the fifth one, my wife pointed out that we had all the passive income we would need for retirement—and it would continue to grow in the years to come. So we stopped acquiring properties, and by the time I retired, we had more wealth and income from our real estate investments than from our combined tax-deferred retirement accounts.

Two critical aspects of handling real estate investments are keeping good records and working with a CPA with business experience. Understanding the true tax implications of depreciation of your investment properties is an important part of the process and planning. I'll share ways to take advantage of some of the other tax benefits too.

My advice is normally to never sell your investment property, since you bought it for the long haul. But sometimes it's necessary and you can use the sale of one property to fund the purchase of a larger one. You'll understand how to sell it and strategies for avoiding taxes when you can.

You'll want to keep this book and re-read certain chapters every time you get ready to purchase another piece of investment real estate—but understand that you don't need all your ducks in a row before you make your first offer. I provide 10 steps for you to use in getting started *today*. Your first purchase will be the scariest/hardest, but they get easier from there. With the knowledge I'm sharing in this book, what are you waiting for? Get started today!

Introduction

I left my 20-year general surgical practice at age 51, only 12 years after buying my first apartment complex. By then, my real estate investments were producing more passive income than I was spending. I no longer needed to work. During those 12 years of real estate investing, utilizing about 10-15 hours a month of my time, I was able to create more wealth and passive income than I had in 20 years of investing my surgical income. In fact, only a few years after my first apartment purchase, I noticed I was building more wealth in real estate each year than I was earning as a full-time surgeon.

So many doctors asked me how I did it. They wanted passive income too, but didn't realize it was possible to invest in real estate and practice medicine full time. Many were worried about what would happen if they suddenly lost their jobs, as they had seen happen to other physicians. They were worried about the massive pile of debt they had accumulated. Some wanted to get out of medicine. All of them wanted long-term, passive income to protect their families and were not sure they could create it while working as a busy professional.

Through many conversations by the water cooler, I realized that what was holding people back was misinformation: myths about how time-consuming, expensive, and risky it is to invest in real estate.

There was also a general lack of information about how to get started. This book will walk you through it step by step and teach you how to become a successful real estate investor, even while living the busy life of a professional.

I'm going to tell you my story, with real numbers, and show you how I did it. So many books offer hypothetical property purchases as examples and most readers are not convinced it will really happen that way. It's hard to argue with the actual numbers, so I will bare my soul in hopes that you will see how you can do it also.

HOW I STARTED

In 2001, eight years after leaving residency, my wife and I bought our first piece of investment property that was unrelated to my medical practice. This was the first of several real estate purchases that put us on a fast track to financial freedom.

Over the next few years, we accumulated five small apartment complexes, containing a total of 64 rental units. I was the manager and my wife was the bookkeeper. Together, we managed those apartments for 12 years while I was a full-time general surgeon in private practice and my wife was a stay-at-home mother to our two boys.

Real estate investing is not a difficult task, when done correctly. Most doctors have both the time and the ability to own a real estate business on the side. They lack only a little guidance and the willingness to take the first step.

Most people are so worried about the amount of time they mistakenly think it will take to manage a single-family home rental that they would never venture into managing an apartment complex. In reality, managing 64 units doesn't take anywhere near the time and effort they guessed it would take.

There are so many mistaken perceptions about owning rental real estate. Someone will hear of my properties and feel the need to tell me they wouldn't want to unclog a toilet on Thanksgiving. In these conversations, you would be surprised how often a toilet causes the hypothetical problem and the holiday is Thanksgiving. Why people feel obliged to tell me this is an interesting phenomenon.

My thoughts were usually something like, "If they only knew how much money I was making in my sleep, they would be happy to fix an occasional toilet." In reality, emergencies like that are rare and I'm not the one who fixes them when they do happen.

MY REAL ESTATE INVESTMENTS IN RETIREMENT

Today I still have four of those original five apartment complexes, totaling 55 units. These properties produce sufficient cash flow to cover my wife's and my living expenses during our retirement years with an income that continues to grow with inflation every year. Our real estate has also created significant income for some of our family members as a bonus.

Our lifestyle has changed and we are now traveling more than 50% of the year. We no longer manage our real estate ourselves since it would be difficult from a cruise ship off the coast of Brazil, from our motor home on Route 66, or while backpacking across Spain with our phones on airplane mode. (Although some people do long-distance management routinely.)

It is ironic that while I was working full time, I had the time to manage our properties. But now that I am retired/repurposed, I am not home enough to manage the properties effectively.

Most people assume that when they retire from their jobs, they will have the time to become a property manager. For me, the opposite was true. Only when I was a busy professional did I have the time to manage my properties.

Our other investments include a 401(k) from my practice, traditional IRAs for both my wife and me, a health savings account, a 403(b) account from my residency years, and a partnership in two medical buildings. We are not yet old enough for Social Security benefits or Medicare.

The wealth we accumulated from real estate has eclipsed all of our retirement savings during my surgery career, even while going through one of the biggest real estate busts in history, starting in the late 2000s. My real estate cash flow and appreciation has been taxed very little, as is the nature of wealth generated by real estate. Most would say we live a very comfortable lifestyle.

I was always an entrepreneur, even as a teenager. Now I am a repurposed general surgeon who has morphed into an author, speaker, and financial coach for doctors and other high-income professionals. This book is the next step in my journey to pass on the knowledge I've obtained over the years, so you won't have to figure it all out yourself.

YOU HAVE EVERYTHING TO GAIN

Come with me on this journey and you will be able to start your own real estate empire with confidence. Don't listen to the naysayers. Don't listen to people who don't own any rental real estate. And please don't take any advice from a reluctant landlord who got stuck with a house she couldn't sell and decided to rent it out for a while. They rarely have a good go of it and don't have the knowledge to teach you how to become a successful real estate investor.

If you follow the advice in the following pages, you will have the necessary tools to become a successful real estate investor. My grandparents did it with little education and a job that produced little income. Neither graduated from high school, and Grandpa worked in a plywood mill while Grandma stayed home with the kids. I did it with a lot of education and a job that produced a high income and required a lot of my time. And with a little guidance, you can do it too. There is no reason you cannot follow in the footsteps of those who have done it before you.

If you are anxious to get started, read through the table of contents and jump to the chapter you need the most right now— and that might be the last chapter on the ten steps to getting started. After that you can go back and read the rest of the book. Read it at least twice. You should also go back to the sections on assessing your real estate before every purchase. Then you will lessen the chance of buying the wrong property.

Regardless of your current income level or what the current real estate market looks like, it's always the right time to buy a good piece of real estate. And yes, even a busy professional can become a successful real estate investor.

"Now, one thing I tell everyone is learn about real estate. Repeat after me: real estate provides the highest returns, the greatest values, and the least risk."

— Armstrong Williams

Chapter 1

WHY REAL ESTATE IS YOUR BEST INVESTMENT

You can invest for future income in many ways. Most conservative investments grow with time. Some investments grow faster than others, like stocks compared to bonds. Some are taxed more than others, like a passbook savings account compared to a retirement account. A few investments will even lose money, like the restaurant I was once a partner in. Some require lots of effort—like your job—while others require almost no effort, like buying treasury bills. Real estate lies in the sweet spot of investment opportunities. It has cash flow, appreciation, and great tax advantages, and it requires relatively little time commitment.

I should define what real estate investing means for the purpose of this book. I'm talking about owning something you can walk up to and hit with a hammer. It is tangible. You are the owner. You get all of the profit and all of the tax breaks. It is not a piece of paper denoting a sector stock like a REIT (real estate investment trust). It is not loaning money so someone else can be a real estate investor like crowdfunding. It is not an anonymous partnership like a syndication would be. It is full ownership and control of a piece of property. It's the real deal.

As the owner, you are in charge. You set the rules. You make the profit. You take the lumps if you mess up. You get all the tax breaks. You become the king of an empire.

Let's go over some of the reasons real estate is such a great investment.

CASH FLOW

This is the single most important aspect of real estate investing. The cash flow will change your life. It is the cash flow you will be spending in your retirement and that will allow you to retire in the first place.

So what is cash flow? It is the money left over after you take in all the rent and pay all the bills and account for future expenses. It is the money you have available to spend on *you*. It is the spendable profits of your real estate business.

$$\text{Income} - \text{Expenses} - \text{Contingencies} = \text{Cash Flow}$$

The amount of cash flow you have when you initially purchase a property is not the important factor; it will grow with time as the rent increases and the debt decreases. It is only important that the cash flow from each property is positive. A negative cash flow would mean the expenses exceeded the income, which is not good.

> The property must earn more money than it costs to own. Income must exceed expenses. In other words, cash flow must be positive.

Never consider a property with a negative cash flow unless there is some extenuating circumstance you can quickly correct to create a positive cash flow.

If you buy properties with a negative cash flow, you will be limited to owning only as many properties as your other earned income could supplement. For example, if the negative cash flow was $100 a month, and you have an available excess income of $500 a month from your job, you could only own five properties before you would run out of money to supplement them (at a negative $100 each).

On the other hand, if you consider properties with a $100 positive cash flow, you can own an unlimited number of these.

Each additional purchase will put another $100 a month into your pocket.

Over time, rents tend to increase. With each rent increase comes a corresponding increase in cash flow. So the longer you own a property, the greater your cash flow becomes.

Over time, mortgages tend to get paid down by the tenants and eventually are paid off. With each mortgage retirement, your cash flow increases significantly.

> *Borrowing money is a good idea when someone else is paying the loan.*

The combination of mortgage pay-down and rent increases creates cash flow that keeps up with inflation. So even after you retire and begin living on your real estate cash flow, your income will continue to grow each year. Now that's the kind of investment we all want to have.

ASSET APPRECIATION

The value of property has generally increased over time. You may see dips here and there, but overall, you can assume the value of your real estate investment will grow. This alone will make you a multimillionaire.

Asset appreciation alone can make you a multimillionaire.

According to the most recently published data from the United States Census Bureau (housing census), the median United States home value has increased dramatically over the last several decades.

MEDIAN HOME VALUE APPRECIATION

Year	Actual Values ($)	Adjusted to 2000 Values ($)
1940	2,938	30,600
1950	7,354	44,600
1960	11,900	58,600
1970	17,000	65,300
1980	47,200	93,400
1990	79,100	101,100
2000	119,600	119,600
2010*	163,000	-
2019*	226,000	-
*Zillow Home Values		

(You can see the full report by state at https://www.census.gov/hhes/www/housing/census/historic/values.html)

The median home value has continued to grow since 2000. I turned to Zillow to see what they had to say for more recent home values and found the last two values since 2000, included in the chart.

(You can see the full Zillow report here: https://www.zillow.com/home-values/)

Unfortunately, we don't get to spend our appreciation. This is why it is less valuable than cash flow. But if you were to sell a property, gift it to charity, or pass it on to your heirs, then this appreciated value comes into play.

"Buy land, they're not making it anymore."

— Mark Twain

LEVERAGE

This is a great aspect of real estate. You can purchase a property with only a small amount of money, or even with no money, borrow the rest, and put the property into your portfolio. Then it begins to grow in value as it appreciates and will start to spin cash flow into your pocket.

This growth is not based on how much money you invested into the property. The growth is based on the total value of the property, which has a way of greatly increasing the return on investment.

For example, if I buy a property worth $100,000 and use $10,000 of my own money to do it, I control an asset worth 10 times the value of my investment. The equity is only $10,000, but the property as an investment will behave as if it is worth $100,000—its actual value.

If the property has a net operating income of $6,000, and the mortgage costs $5,000 a year, then the property is spinning off a cash flow of $1,000 a year. My $10,000 is earning $1,000 a year for a 10% return on my investment—tax-free. (Depreciation will make it tax-free and I will discuss that later.)

If the property appreciates at 3% per year, it will grow $3,000 in value by the end of the first year and this increase will also not be taxed. That makes an additional 30% return.

Cash flow plus appreciation will return $4,000 for my $10,000 investment. That comes to a 40% tax-free return on my investment.

If I did not use leverage to buy the property and paid the entire $100,000 up front, I would have invested the full value of the property. Since I would not have the $5,000 a year mortgage payment, I would receive $6,000 a year in cash flow and $3,000 in appreciation for a total of $9,000 in annual return. That would be a 9% return on my investment, most of which would be tax-free. The effect of the leverage is to create a return that is about five times greater, after taxes, than if I had no leverage.

THE EFFECT OF LEVERAGE ON ROI

	Leverage	No Leverage
Property Value	100,000	100,000
Investment	10,000	100,000
Mortgage Amount	90,000	0
Net Operating Income (NOI)	6,000	6,000
Annual Mortgage Payment	5,000	0

	Leverage	No Leverage
Cash Flow	1,000	6,000
Appreciation, 3%	3,000	3,000
Total Return	4,000	9,000
Return on Investment (ROI)	40%	9%

This one little benefit—leverage—can create a substantial amount of wealth.

Leverage allows you to create substantial wealth with a relatively small investment.

For a relatively small investment, I can put a $100,000 piece of property into my investment portfolio. Then, all the future cash flow and appreciation from that investment will be mine.

Getting these properties into my pocket for future growth has a powerful compounding effect that hugely overshadows anything I can do with the investment in my 401(k)—which has no leverage.

"Landlords grow rich in their sleep."

— John Stuart Mill

DEPRECIATION

I love this nice little benefit of investment real estate. The government has determined that the useful life of a rental building is 27.5 years. This is really an arbitrary number, only useful in determining your taxes, since rental properties can last for a century or more if you take good care of them.

You cannot depreciate the value of the land, only the buildings. So with the $100,000 property we discussed above, the land might be worth $20,000 and the building $80,000. It doesn't matter how old the building is, either. The 27.5 years starts *for me* when I buy the building.

This $80,000 building has a depreciation of $2,909.09 each year for the next 27.5 years, which I will take as a write-off on my profits each year. So, since the $1,000 I made in cash flow is less than my $2,909.09 write-off for depreciation, it will not be taxed. I will then have an extra $1,909.09 to carry over to help shelter next year's profits. There are other things that go into this calculation that I left off for simplicity. For the nonleveraged option, the depreciation will make $2,909.09 of the $6,000 of cash flow not taxed.

> ## The depreciation tax write-off makes real estate investing more effective at putting money in your pocket than any other investment option.

Because of this depreciation tax write-off, the money you earn in real estate is more effective at putting money into your pocket than any other investment option that does not have depreciation. It's almost like having another Roth IRA.

FLEXIBILITY

Real estate investments have tremendous flexibility. Usually, in order to get good tax advantages on your retirement investments like a 401(k) would have, you must follow a lot of rules laid down by the IRS—for example, not using the money before reaching the age 59½ or being forced to begin withdrawing the money at age 70½.

Since investment property is not kept in any special account (IRA, 401(k), 403(b), HSA, 529), there are no special rules to follow. You can sell it whenever you want, use the cash flow to buy a new car without penalties, reinvest the cash flow to improve the property, or even buy another property.

Real estate earns investment income, in a tax-protected manner, without a lot of pesky restrictions. If retiring before age 59½ is what you have in mind, owning investment real estate could be a very important piece of the puzzle. The money is available at any age and still gets tax advantages.

There's no concern about what day of the year it is, either. Many tax-protected accounts have restrictions as to how much you can contribute each calendar year, or what has to be done before December 31 or April 15. For example, in 2019 I can only contribute a maximum of $6,000 to my IRA before April 15 of 2020.

With real estate, I can invest anytime and for any amount of money. There are no artificial ceilings placed on real estate investments. I can buy a million-dollar property today and another one every month, if I want. Or I can buy one $100,000 property only once in my entire life. I have full flexibility as to when, where, and how I invest in real estate, and I can still get the tax advantages.

I left my partnership at age 51 and worked part time in locums until I retired from my general surgery career at age 54, when I could only access some of my IRA money without penalty. I followed the Substantially Equal Periodic Payment rules, IRS rule 72(t), to get at my money penalty-free. But I didn't have any rules to follow for my real estate investment money (for a guide on how to utilize IRS rule 72(t), see my blog at https://drcorysfawcett.com/guide-to-taking-substantially-equal-periodic-payments-sepp-from-your-ira-before-age-59/).

You can use real estate cash flow money without any rules or restrictions.

Because I had full use of my real estate cash flow, I could retire with the same lifestyle I had during my working years. I was able to retire at a relatively young age because I had real estate income that was not subject to government restrictions. I can spend all of it to live on if I want. For me, the real estate earns more cash flow than I spend each year, so I don't think I will run out of money anytime soon.

I could not have retired at age 54 if I had to rely only on what I could withdraw from my retirement plans without penalties. That flexibility makes real estate a great investment.

IT'S A BUSINESS

There are huge tax advantages to owning a business, and doctors today are losing those advantages as medicine transitions to an employment model. By starting a real estate business, you can get back some of those lost advantages that employees do not enjoy.

This business creates a vehicle for using deductions. I covered depreciation already, but it is just the beginning. If you own a business, you can write off so many things on your taxes that are not available to you as an employee of someone else's business.

WRITE-OFFS

If you are the manager of the property, you will need some tools to do the job. These are often tools you need at your own home. Anytime you can turn a tool into a tax write-off, it is a bonus. Some examples include a cell phone, camera, utility trailer, vehicle to pull a utility trailer, leaf blower, tools for minor home repairs, gloves, yard-working tools, lawn mower, computer, internet service, second line on home phone, answering machine, ladders, cleaning supplies, home office, and anything else you use to take care of your rentals.

Unlike your personal expenses, these real estate business write-offs are not limited to that amount exceeding the standard deduction of $24,000, if married and filing jointly (the current standard deduction at the time of writing).

In your business, every deductible dollar gets deducted.

For example, due to the standard deduction, not all of the interest you pay for your home mortgage is deductible. The first $24,000 doesn't count. But your investment property interest is fully deductible and is not affected by the standard deduction.

HIRE YOUR FAMILY

Since you own a business, you can employ your family. There are great tax advantages to having your children work in your business. If you hire your kids as minors, they may not have to pay Social Security tax, Medicare tax (FICA), or federal unemployment tax (FUTA). They also get their own standard deduction of $12,000, making the first $12,000 they earn federal tax-free. The child can use the money to fund their Roth IRA with pre-tax dollars, since they have zero tax liability. You also get to take a business deduction for the money you pay your kids, which you might have given them anyway without a deduction, which decreases your tax bill.

It makes remarkably good sense to hire your children and pay them at least enough to make a $6,000 Roth IRA contribution. Imagine the financial impact of a child earning compound interest through age 65 on money that will never be taxed.

If your child worked for you each year and earned $6,000 ($500 per month) and put it into their Roth IRA from ages 12 through 20, they would have contributed for nine years with a total contribution of $54,000. If they never put another dollar into their IRA and earned an 8% return over their lifetime, at age 65 they would have over $2,800,000—which will never be taxed.

Because a real estate investment is a business, you can have an additional retirement plan. As an employee, your retirement investment options are limited to only what your employer offers. If you add a real estate business, you can create additional retirement plan accounts and put away even more money in tax-protected accounts. With additional retirement plans, you can give yourself the same benefit you gave your child with their Roth IRA.

PASSIVE INCOME

Real estate is a passive form of income. I love this feature. It is very important to generate passive income that protects you from job loss and provides for a nice retirement. When I was younger, I took an active role in the management of my real estate. I was the manager. This was a part-time job that I enjoyed doing about 10-15 hours a month. It was a nice change of pace from what I did as a physician.

But when I retired from medicine, I wanted to travel a lot. I couldn't manage my real estate investments from Europe, so I hired a property management company to do the work. So you can choose your involvement level, from running it all yourself to merely cashing the checks. I do spend a little time keeping an eye on the management, but even that is optional. Because I am still the business owner, I can still take advantage of all the write-offs I listed above.

The cash flow is running right into my pocket and is increasing each year as rents rise and mortgages fall. The property continues to appreciate in value. Both of these things are happening while I am somewhere else in the world. Today I am writing these words while wearing my bathrobe, sitting in my motorhome in an RV park in Las Vegas, Nevada. I will be joining my mother and her friend at a couple of shows later in the day. Despite being 770 miles from home, the property is still spinning off profits for me to buy show tickets and pay for this RV space.

ANYONE CAN DO IT

I think this is the most important point of all—anyone can do it. I didn't need a special license to buy my first investment property. I didn't need a permit to manage it myself. The knowledge I needed to be a real estate investor is readily available. I can read books in the library or find articles on the internet. As a result of what I've learned, you can read this book.

My grandparents hadn't completed high school when they started investing in real estate. They would save up a little money and use it for a down payment on a very inexpensive rental house. Then the rental income from the tenants would pay off any remaining mortgage over the years. They did this about a dozen times.

My grandfather did not have a contractor's license, but he was able to fix things in the rentals as needed. He was not a roofing contractor, but he put on new roofs. He was not a journeyman plumber, but he could fix a dripping faucet. He was not an electrician, but he could replace a faulty light switch. You get the picture.

My grandparents could easily have said they didn't have the education or the money to get into real estate. They never said or thought that. They just went out and did it. They often took me along as a teen to help them fix things and I suspect that is where I got the notion to try it for myself.

Everyone else in the family saw what my grandparents did, just like me. But no one else became a real estate investor. I realized that if my grandparents could do it, with an eighth-grade education and a millworker's income, then anyone could do it. Even me!

If my grandparents could become real estate investors with a 40-hour-per-week job, and I could do it as a busy professional with a 60-plus-hour-per-week job, and millions of others could do it as well, then so can you. What are you waiting for?

"Buying real estate is not only the best way, the quickest way, the safest way, but the only way to become wealthy."

— Marshal Field

Chapter 2

THE REAL ESTATE INVESTOR VERSUS THE RELUCTANT LANDLORD

I grew up watching my grandparents build their real estate portfolio. They were not wealthy people. I was the oldest grandson and as I mentioned, I often went with them to help make repairs on their properties.

I learned all kinds of interesting skills. Roofing, plumbing, carpentry, electrical, and painting were some of the good ones. One skill I never want to use again is cleaning out an underground septic tank. Some skills are best left unused.

After my grandfather died, when I was 15 years old, I noticed my grandmother didn't need to get a job to make ends meet. She was living on the proceeds of the seven rental houses she owned free and clear. She was also managing them herself and spent very little time doing manager tasks. She had plenty of time to play and travel.

I decided that someday I would do the same thing she did and invest in rental real estate. But why was I the only one in the family to follow her lead? Couldn't they see the same benefits I saw? Didn't they want good cash flow in their retirement years? Didn't they want to have enough passive income to be able to quit their jobs?

I asked a few of them over the years why they didn't own any investment real estate and here are some of their responses:

"Your grandmother is a slumlord."

"Those places are dumps."

"She should tear down those houses."

"I don't know how to fix things."

"Her tenants are always tearing up those houses."

"I don't have time to take care of rentals."

"I don't have any money to buy rentals."

"I have other places I invest my money."

"I don't want to be tied to staying home on the weekends."

"She wastes a lot of time working on those places."

"I want my free time to be free."

And of course, "I don't want to unplug someone else's toilet on Thanksgiving."

It was an interesting pattern. Everyone had something to gripe about concerning owning rental property. Not one person said anything about how Grandma didn't need a job and had the time and money to travel. I don't think anyone realized she was a millionaire. I don't recall ever hearing a single positive statement about my grandmother owning rental property.

IT'S A QUESTION OF PERSPECTIVE

How is it that people could only see one side of the story? Only the negative prevailed. Were they jealous that she didn't need to work? Were they jaded by some past experience? What made them so negative? Every endeavor has its pluses and minuses. Why are only the minuses seen when discussing rental property?

I thought about this in relation to my becoming a doctor. When I talked about this dream, everyone was positive, happy, and excited for my future. No one said anything like the following:

"You'll have to go in at night to fix some drunk who crashed his car."

"Don't you realize how many of your kids' events you will miss?"

"The suicide rate for doctors is very high."

"You'll get burned out."

"Why would you volunteer for a 60-hour-a-week job?"

"Don't you realize how long you have to go to school for that?"

"People are always dying on you."

"You're going to catch diseases, treating all those sick people."

"You don't want to do that. You'll get sued."

"Why would you want to live your life tied to a pager?"

"Doctors have a high divorce rate."

"You'll never get your student loans paid off."

Even to this day, I'm not quite sure how only the negative things come up in conversation if I mention investing in real estate and only the positive things come up when I say I'm a physician.

I only had one person ever discourage me from becoming a physician, a professor in college who was teaching computer programming. I was a natural at programming and he really liked my work. When he found out I was pre-med, he said this:

"What a waste. Anyone who can get good grades can become a physician. Not everyone can program like you do. Don't waste all this talent by becoming a physician. You'll work longer hours and never make the money you could make in programming."

When someone asks me what I do for a living, if I say I'm a surgeon, I get all kinds of praise. If I say I'm an author who has published several award-winning and best-selling books, I get some wows. But if I tell them I own rental real estate, I get a long list of reasons why they would never do that.

THE RELUCTANT LANDLORD

After much thinking on the subject, I have concluded that the problem is the "reluctant landlord." This is the person who bought a house to live in and then moved. The housing market was down when they were forced to move and they couldn't sell the house without taking a loss, so they became a reluctant landlord and rented out the house until they could sell it for a profit.

These people never wanted to become a landlord in the first place. They did not buy the property with the thought of renting it for a profit. And they didn't know anything about being a landlord. They were not real estate investors and they really didn't have the information they needed to become successful.

Here is a list of some of the differences between a reluctant landlord and a real estate investor.

	Reluctant Landlord	Investor
Bought with profit in mind	No	Yes
Lives near the property	Unlikely	Likely
Is making a profit	No	Yes
Wants the investment	No	Yes
Understands real estate	No	Yes
Understands real estate investing	No	Yes
Studies real estate	No	Yes
Is in it for the long haul	No	Yes
Likes owning the property	No	Yes
Speaks well of real estate investing	No	Yes
Ready to buy another one	No	Yes
Having a good experience	No	Yes
Wants to be a real estate investor	No	Yes
Has good tenants	Maybe	Usually
Wants to build equity	No	Yes
Willing to pay a manager	No	Yes
Sees benefit in the mortgage	No	Yes
Can afford major repairs	Maybe	Usually
Sees long term benefits	No	Yes
Wants out ASAP	Yes	No

It's no wonder the experiences of reluctant landlords give real estate investment a bad name. They rarely speak well of real estate investing. They have never been a real estate investor but think they are because they own a rental property. They may talk like they know something about real estate investing. They had a bad experience once in a situation that makes them think they are real estate investors. They then badmouth this to everyone. "Tenants just tear everything up." "Being a landlord is such a headache." "I'm tired of getting called at night." "Rentals just don't make any money." "Being a landlord is just too risky."

How would the reluctant landlord concept play out in a different area? What if your friend asked you to go with her tomorrow to run a half-marathon, but you have never trained for or thought about long-distance running? You might reluctantly agree and show up in shorts and sneakers, thinking you are in decent shape so it should be OK. After a few miles, you regret the decision to do this. You can hardly breathe, your feet hurt, your knees hurt, your hips hurt, you've got that crazy side ache, and your back hurts. You do finish the 13-mile race, right after sunset, and you walked much of it.

The next day you hurt all over and have blisters on your feet. A friend asks you how it went and you have nothing positive to say about the experience. You try to convince them they should never take up running for the rest of their life.

Did you give running a fair trial? No, you didn't. You should have done some research about how to train for endurance running. You should have learned about nutrition and hydration for endurance athletes. You should have trained for this, starting with short distances and working your way up.

Your buddy, on the other hand, is talking up the race—how great it felt to finish in the top 10 in her age group, how much better she feels since she took up running. She can list the health benefits she is experiencing.

One of you is a runner and has great things to say about running. The other is a reluctant participant in a single running event. The reluctant runner did not have a good experience and spreads the news accordingly.

You cannot walk onto the starting line of a half-marathon with no preparation and have a positive experience. Without the proper training, the experience will not be good. There will be pain and blisters. The reluctant runner also has no business telling other people what they should do to successfully run a half-marathon, because they don't know how to do that.

This is the same effect as the reluctant landlord versus the real estate investor. If one is forced into becoming a reluctant landlord, they shouldn't use that experience to decide what it is like to be a real estate investor. They do not know how to be a real estate investor.

If you are or were a reluctant landlord, tell people about your experience and clarify that you didn't know what you were doing and didn't want to be doing it. Let them know you were a reluctant landlord. When people ask you, just say you don't have any experience as a real estate investor, but you were a reluctant landlord once and that is not the right way to go about owning real estate.

Since you are reading this book, I know you want to become a real estate investor. So be careful where you get your advice. Steer clear of the reluctant landlord. You can distinguish this with one question: How did you acquire your rental property?

If you determine the person you are talking with is a reluctant landlord, you should be polite, but realize you will not be using their advice. But it is fun to listen to their story and avoid repeating their mistakes.

HOW REAL ESTATE INVESTORS DO IT

Get advice from someone who has actually done what you want to do. Seek out those who have several pieces of property similar to the kind you want to buy. If you want single-family homes, find someone who rents out several of them. If you want commercial property, find someone with several of them. If you want to buy apartments like I did, seek out someone who owns several apartments and is doing well. Talk to other investors and see what they have to say. They are usually happy to give you their knowledge, as they are proud to tell you their story, especially if you are interested in joining them.

Real estate investing is a skill that is easily learned if you will just seek out the knowledge.

GET ADVICE FROM SUCCESSFUL INVESTORS

You also want to avoid the person who has heard or read about real estate investing but has not done it themselves. I see this a lot in blogs and comments on blog articles. Many people with no actual experience are ready to tell you how it should be done. They will be of no help to you.

After you have been a real estate investor for a while, you will be able to spot these guys fairly easily. But as a newbie, be very careful who you listen to. Not all advice is good advice and people who have only read about it are not likely to give you good advice.

This is one of the bad things about anonymous bloggers. You really don't know what they have for experience. If you don't trust the unknown person who calls you and tells you he is from Microsoft and your computer is infected, don't trust other anonymous advice. Be sure you understand who is giving you the advice and what their experience has been.

Most of all, don't listen to the person in the cafeteria who knows a guy whose grand-step-neighbor-in-law had a bad experience with a rental. Naysayers rarely can provide you with help about anything. So stop listening to them, go find yourself a good piece of property to buy, and get started building your real estate empire.

"Please, tell me more about how you're an expert in real estate because you watch HGTV."

— Someecards.com

Chapter 3

HOW I PURCHASED MY FIRST APARTMENT COMPLEX WITH NO MONEY DOWN

PREPARATION PHASE

If you've read book two in my series, *The Doctors Guide to Eliminating Debt,* you know the 1990s were significant for me, as I was getting deep into and then out of debt. By 2001, I was zeroing in on becoming debt-free. My final house payment was in October of that year.

My wife, Carolyn, and I began to discuss what we would do with all the money we would have left over every month, once we became debt-free. After the final debt payment was made, we would have around $10,000 a month in available income that used to go toward getting out of debt using the snowball method. We needed a plan for this money, before it started burning a hole in our pocket. We were worried that if we didn't develop a plan, the money would just get frittered away on stuff.

We settled on investing the money in real estate. We were already maxing out retirement plan contributions in protected accounts, including my 401(k) and both of our IRA accounts. This new money would be used to buy investment property and follow in my grandparents' footsteps.

I started looking into real estate investing. I bought some books. The internet wasn't much help at the time, so I just walked into a bookstore and picked out a few books from the real estate investing shelf. Some were good and some, not so much.

Then one night when I was up late at the hospital, I saw an infomercial. A guy named Carleton Sheets was pushing a real estate course to teach me everything I needed to know about the process. That sounded like just what I needed. I bought the course.

The course description was "How to buy your first home or investment property with NO DOWN PAYMENT. Step-by-step manual." It turned out to be a great course that taught everything about real estate, including how to do it with no money down.

The course advised to start small, using what you are familiar with, and work your way up as you get more comfortable. Most people are comfortable with buying a single-family home as they have done it before, so he suggested starting there.

I'm kind of a go big or go home type of guy. I started shopping for small apartment complexes.

About that time, the house next door went on the market and I got a new neighbor. He used to be a real estate investor in southern California. He sold everything and took the profits and moved to Oregon, right next to me. He was now using his knowledge to sell real estate as a broker. We talked about what I wanted to do and he, as a past investor, knew just what I was looking for.

Serendipitously, I had found a good realtor to do my searching for me. A short time later he gave me a call. There was a 31-unit apartment complex for sale that seemed to fit my parameters. The asking price was $1,300,000.

EXPLORATION PHASE

By now I had learned enough to know how to determine the value of an investment property. I ran the numbers (I'll explain how to do this in a later chapter) and it seemed like I could make it work. In fact, I thought I could buy the property with no money down.

I asked for a meeting with the owner so we could walk through the property and get a feel for what was there. He had been managing it for a long time himself, so he knew the ins and outs of the place. As we walked the property, I not only learned about the property, but I also learned about the man who was selling it.

He was a nice guy who was ready to retire and sail around the world in his sailboat. It had been a long-time dream of his. I asked him why he didn't get a manager and use the cash flow to finance his sailing adventure.

He initially had that same idea and hired a guy to manage the place for him. Since he had no mortgage, there was plenty of profit to pay for management and cover all his travel expenses. He didn't want a property management company—he didn't like them—but an individual who could do the job like he had done was just what he needed.

One day during his travels he called back home to check on the place. He called a long-term tenant whom he knew very well to get a feel for how things were going. The tenant was surprised to hear from him.

It seems the manager had told everyone that the owner had died in an accident during his travels and left the apartment to his friend, the manager. The manager had the place up for sale.

Of course, the owner interrupted his travel immediately and came home to get rid of the manager. I'm not sure if the manager could have successfully made the sale, but with no mortgage and a missing owner, he apparently thought it was possible.

After that, the owner did not want to take another chance and had decided to sell the place and live off the interest. It was my lucky day.

I learned more about his needs. He wanted a steady income to live on. He needed enough money to pay off his house and buy a new boat, as well as outfit it. He told me what those things would cost. He could not make a deal without at least enough cash to do those things.

THE OFFER

After getting a good feel for the property and for the owner's needs, I went home to craft an offer for the property. I showed the offer to my realtor to write up and told him I would make the offer to the owner myself, in person.

My realtor said that wasn't how things were done. The offer should be given to the other realtor to take to the owner. But I held firm and told him to make arrangements for us to present the offer in person.

As my realtor looked over the offer, he said there was no way they would take it. But I thought differently. I was offering everything the seller asked for, but it was less than his asking price.

Sometimes it is thinking differently that makes the difference.

My offer was to give the seller enough cash to pay off his house, buy the boat and outfit it for the trip with a little extra spending money. I also asked him to carry the papers on a 30-year mortgage at 7.75%, about the current prime rate, and I would make those monthly payments to him so he could do his traveling. There was even a penalty if I paid it off early.

He took the offer as I made it with no counteroffer. How can you counter if you get everything you want? The total offer was $150,000 less than the asking price, but he got everything he needed.

My realtor later told me if he had thought the owner would take that offer, he would have bought the place himself.

From the seller's end of the deal, he got enough cash to do what he needed and a long-term commitment for monthly income. From my end of the deal, I bought the apartment with no money down and got cash back at closing.

It is best not to tell the seller you are buying with no money down. Sellers can be frightened off by this as they may not understand what is happening. This is true even if you are not using seller financing.

Essentially, I was paid to take over the property. How can that be if he got a lot of cash? Because both ends of the deal are independent. Just because he got cash doesn't mean it came from me. None of the money came from me, which is the essence of no-money-down deals. It is also known as 100% financing.

Here's how the deal was structured from my end, as a no-money-down deal:

- $850,000 first mortgage to the seller at 7.75%, with interest-only monthly payments of $5,489.58 for five years. I was allowed to make extra principle payments at my discretion that did not exceed 10% of the outstanding balance for any calendar year. After five years, the remaining balance would be amortized over 25 years, creating a new minimum monthly payment for the remainder of the loan period.

- $100,000 second mortgage from my realtor/neighbor at 8%, interest only with a balloon in five years.

- $180,550 unsecured signature loan from my bank.

- $20,000 private loan from a relative at 8%.

- Total of $1,150,550 borrowed for a $1,150,000 purchase price.

Then the seller provided some concessions we found in the inspection. In the end, the seller's contribution was greater than our total closing costs and we walked away with a check for $2,297.63.

Here's how the no-money-down deal looked from the seller's end:

- $300,000 cash down payment, 26% down.

- $850,000 owner carry at 7.75% with minimum monthly payments of $5,489.58 for what would essentially be the rest of his life.

With this deal, I had calculated a positive cash flow of a few thousand dollars a year. So why were we willing to buy something with 100% financing? Isn't that risky?

I didn't think the deal was risky, for several reasons:

1.   The seller had not raised rent in a long time and rents were way under market rate. In fact, the seller hated paying taxes so much that when he paid off his mortgage on the property a few years before, he lowered everyone's rent to avoid paying income taxes. It made him plenty of money to live on without having to pay additional taxes. We could easily raise rents quite a bit to increase income and cash flow. I checked around to see what similar apartment units rented for in the area and knew I had room to raise rents.

2.   As I mentioned, we were about to pay off our last personal debt and would have an extra $10,000 a month to invest. Our plan was to use this extra money to pay off the $300,000 down payment of cash we had given the seller in the deal (owed to the bank, the broker, and a relative). That would leave us with only the

main mortgage and a nice monthly income. We were essentially paying the down payment over time.

3. The real estate market was solid in our area. This was a bread-and-butter property containing units with two beds and one bath, in good shape with a middle-range rent rate.

4. We purchased the place on the last day of the month. Rent was due for all units the next day, so we were to collect $12,500 to put in the bank within a week of the purchase.

You might ask, wasn't it a big risk for the seller to take a no-money-down deal? First off, the seller didn't know it was a no-money-down deal. He only knew he got $300,000 cash and an owner-carry first mortgage worth $5,489.58 a month for life.

If I was to default on the loan, he would get the property back to sell again and he would keep the $300,000. There was very little risk for him. This was a win-win deal for both of us.

Of note, I have been on both sides of owner financing. I sold a property in 2018 and offered a similar owner-financed deal to the buyer. The buyer gave me a nice down payment of about 40% cash. Their cash came from a 1031 exchange, not out of their pocket, so they had essentially a no-money-down deal. I am carrying the papers for 35 years at a 6% fixed interest rate. Their realtor said my loan terms were very generous. Then I mentioned that the best thing for me would be if they defaulted on the loan. I would get to keep the down payment money and sell the place again to someone else and collect another down payment.

OUR PLAN FOR THE FIRST YEAR: THE LEARNING PHASE

So we were the proud owners of a million-dollar piece of rental real estate. We were in our late 30s and had two boys, aged seven and nine. I worked as a full-time general surgeon and my wife was a stay-at-home mom.

While the property was in escrow, we formed an LLC to own the property. It cost us a few hundred dollars to have our attorney set up the LLC and we put all our later property purchases into it as well. I do not recommend a separate LLC for every property. One is enough.

Our financial plan was to take the extra $10,000 a month we had after paying off our personal debts and apply it using the same snowball method for paying off our real estate business loans (I cover the snowball method in my book *The Doctors Guide to Eliminating Debt*). Eventually, the real estate business would also be debt-free. As each of the down payment loans were paid off, our cash flow would increase.

We knew the rents were too low for the market, but we did not feel good about raising anyone's rent all the way back up to market rate. We also knew that when tenants are paying rent below market rate, it creates a strong incentive for the tenants to stay put. Tenant turnover is expensive.

So we were going to let the rents increase to market rate as people moved out. We also felt it was reasonable for the existing tenants to get some kind of rent increase but not enough to make them mad and move. So we raised everyone's rent by $20 a month. That gave us another $7,440 a year in cash flow.

Each time a tenant moved out, the new tenant paid $80 a month more in rent than the person who left. By the time all the units turned over, that would represent another $30,000 a year in cash flow.

We had not been landlords before. Helping my grandmother take care of her property is not the same as being the owner with all of its responsibility. Reading what to do in a book is also not the same. It is almost like the difference between being a medical student and an attending physician.

So for the first year, we decided to do everything ourselves. We figured we would have a good grasp on what it takes to run those apartments after a year's time. We did it as a family and got the kids involved.

We did all the tenant apartment showing, tenant screening and placement, contracting, repairs, landscape maintenance, room turnovers, painting, plumbing, electrical, and air-conditioning work. If we ran into something we didn't know how to do or couldn't do, we called a professional. This was almost always a plumber or an electrician.

It was not nearly the amount of work I thought it would be. We had a second phone line installed in the house for the property business. My wife answered the phone when I was working and scheduled things.

If someone wanted to see an empty apartment, she tried to schedule that in the evening and I would show it then. Sometimes they couldn't wait until I got off work and Carolyn would show the apartment to them. If the kids were in school, that was best. If they had to come with her, she had them wait in the car while the apartment was shown.

Almost all of the repair work could be scheduled. There are very few true emergencies. Almost all of them involved water, and the emergency ends when the water is shut off.

All unit turnovers were done on weekends, evenings, or my day out of the office. It was actually a fun change of pace for both of us. This included fixing anything that was broken, touch-up painting, shampooing or replacing the carpet, and giving the place a thorough cleaning.

There was other work to do, like collecting the laundry quarters and rent checks and depositing them, paying the bills, keeping accounting records, and doing all the move-in and move-out paperwork.

By the end of the year, we were seasoned property managers running a 31-unit apartment complex. Now we were ready to begin delegating the work.

DELEGATION PHASE

We started removing some of the property management tasks from our plates. By then, rents had increased and there was more money to hire some help.

The first thing we did was hire out the groundskeeping. We asked the gardener we already used for our own house to add the apartment building grounds. He was happy to pick up the work.

Next, we hired someone to do maintenance. We found a contractor who liked to do small jobs. He had recently done a small remodel on our home and he was willing to do the maintenance at the apartments. It would fill in his schedule when he didn't have a small project to do. He could do the little maintenance repairs while going to and from his other jobs, and he took care of all the emergency calls.

This worked out quite well. We continued to be the managers. Carolyn would answer phones, keep the books, and show apartments when I was not free. I placed tenants and collected rents. We did some of the unit turnovers, when we felt like it, and some of them were hired out on an as-needed schedule. The maintenance man helped with the unit turnovers as well.

Carolyn working from home to answer the phone was a big help to us, but was not crucial. The calls she answered could have gone to my voice mail, or we could have hired an answering service to cover the times I was with a patient or in the operating room. There were not many calls.

I recently had the air conditioner in my home quit working. I called the repair shop and left a voicemail. A secretary called me back later and scheduled a time for the repairman to come out and take a look at it. We could have set up a similar system if Carolyn worked outside of the home.

We continued as managers until I left my surgical partnership at the end of 2013 to become a part-time locums surgeon. You can read all about that career move in my third book, *The Doctors Guide to Smart Career Alternatives and Retirement.* Suffice it to say, as we were not in town, we chose to no longer manage the property. But I know owners who do manage their properties from out of town, so even that was doable if we chose to manage from a distance. Phones can be forwarded, and the caller doesn't know where a cell phone they are calling is located.

We chose to turn everything over to a property management company 12 years after our first purchase. When I retired completely, we decided to continue to travel, so we have not gone back to being managers again. We are satisfied with the management company we are using, and I don't suspect we will ever take that job back in the future. Now, I would rather travel.

FINANCIAL GROWTH
NET OPERATING INCOME

When we started out, each unit rented for $385 a month. Today, the new tenants are paying $695 a month when they move in. But we don't get that from all the tenants. As people move, we raise the rent for the new tenant. We don't raise the rent on people who stay in their apartments. So every apartment rents for a slightly different amount based on when the party living there moved in.

Many landlords keep raising everyone's rent, every year. They might also keep the rent the same on every unit. If we did that and everyone was paying market price, then our rental income would go up an additional $36,000 a year. But doing so would cause more tenants to move and increase our unit turnover costs. We don't need to squeeze out every penny, so we don't raise their rent.

Over time, the total rental income has increased, but so have total expenses. Property taxes, water and sewer, garbage, electricity, and the cost of repairs have all gone up as well. We also now have the expense of full-time property management. But rent has gone up faster than expenses, so our profits have been increasing.

When I was working full time as a surgeon, we did not need the income from our real estate investments. We put the profit back into the properties over the years and paid off the loans. We didn't begin to spend any of the profits until I retired from medicine.

The net operating income (NOI), is the rent plus laundry room income minus the expenses to run the place. This income is the money available to pay mortgages. Our NOI for this apartment complex in 2002, the first full tax year, was $110,599. It has grown to $133,516 for 2018. This is a $22,917 increase.

REDUCED DEBT

Over time, we have also paid down our debts. That number is harder to track because we bought other properties later and profits from this first apartment were used to reduce debt on other properties. Had we not purchased any other properties, this property would be completely paid off today. Our original debt was $1,150,550. Seventeen years later it is down to $577,007.

EQUITY

The value of the property started at the purchase price in 2001 of $1,150,000. By 2018, the county assessor's office listed it with a real market value of $2,178,010. We recently sold another property in town and it went for greater than the assessor's real market value, so I suspect this property would do the same.

The net worth, or equity, in the property was originally zero, as it was 100% financed. Seventeen years later, the equity exceeds $1,600,000. My 401(k), which I have had for a longer period and which I invested more money into, is smaller than that figure.

CASH FLOW: PASSIVE INCOME

To me, the most important financial number is the cash flow. That is the money I can spend—the passive income I am living on in my retirement. That is the difference between the NOI and the mortgage payments. Each investor must decide how much positive cash flow is enough to make the deal good for them.

NOI – Mortgage Payment = Cash Flow

The positive cash flow will be used to generate a slush fund for surprise expenses, paying down debt faster, and eventually to live on. For me, with a high income from medicine that I was only living on half of, I had plenty of extra money on hand, so any amount of positive cash flow would work. For others, there might be a higher threshold to entering the deal. Since I planned to keep the property forever, and I knew the cash flow would grow with time, I didn't use any threshold number to make a deal.

Positive cash flow is the key financial component to any successful business.

TAX-FREE INCOME

In our first full tax year of operation, 2002, we had a spendable cash flow of $22,214. Since our depreciation exceeded that figure, it was all tax-free income. In 2018, our spendable cash flow from this property had grown to $107,828. Had this been our only property, it would have no debt today and our spendable cash flow would equal the net operating income (NOI) of $133,516. Of the $107,828 cash flow we received in 2018, only $70,773 of it was taxable. The remaining $37,055 was tax-free income thanks to depreciation.

This one purchase of a 31-unit apartment complex, 17 years ago, was sufficient to fund our retirement by itself. Our living expenses are covered by this cash flow, as we have no personal debt and our kids are grown.

That is not bad for a no-money-down real estate deal set up by a newbie. By the way, a couple of months after I made this purchase, I read another real estate book. In it, they wrote, "And don't believe any of the no-money-down real estate stuff, because it doesn't work."

I'm so glad I didn't read that book first. I went on to buy other properties with no money down and cash back at closing. My son bought a rental single-family home in 2016 with no money down, so it still works.

We went on to buy other small apartments and by 2007, we owned five of them with a total of 64 units rented. One of those units was a nine-plex that was owned in a partnership and was sold in 2018. I referred to this property earlier as the apartment that sold for more than the assessed real market value.

Today we have 55 apartment units in four complexes, all within a couple of miles from our home. We borrowed originally $3,170,000 to acquire these properties, in addition to carrying the mortgage on the one we sold. We still owe $1,702,153 on those loans. We have contributed $448,000 over the years and the tenants have paid down $1,019,847 with their rent payments, which also created our cash flow. Our current equity in these apartments is $2,874,213 (using the tax assessor's real market value of each property, which we feel is a bit low) and we would realize in excess of $3 million easily, if they were sold at the time of this writing.

To sum that up: In addition to our sweat equity, we have contributed $448,000 in cash into our real estate investments, which are now worth in excess of $3,000,000 and provide more than $150,000 of cash flow per year—and climbing. Of that $150,000 we can spend each year, $69,971 of it is taxable and $80,029 is tax-free. It has been 17½ years since we made the first purchase.

To this day, we continue to pay down the real estate debt using the snowball method. Someday it will be a debt-free enterprise. But for now, we will go on traveling the world and spending our real estate cash flow.

"The major fortunes in America have been made in land."

— John D. Rockefeller

Chapter 4

IT IS ALWAYS A GOOD TIME TO BUY INVESTMENT REAL ESTATE

A lot of people ask me if I think now is the right time to buy investment real estate. The answer to that question is always *yes!* You see, it is always a good time to buy investment real estate. It might not always be a good time to sell, but it is always a good time to buy.

The real premise behind this question is that buying investment real estate is *never* about timing the market. Frankly, it is impossible to time the market. We should all have learned that with the stock market. The same is true for the real estate market. There is no way to tell if a market is at the bottom or still dropping. There is no way to tell if a market is at a peak or still climbing. Since there is no way to time the market, stop wasting your time trying. Leave that to the real estate speculators. You want to become a real estate investor.

There is a big difference between real estate speculators and real estate investors.

Let's go back in time and imagine a real estate investor struggling with this question in 1975. I mentioned in chapter 1 that the median home value in 1970 was $17,000 and in 1980 it was $47,200. As of this writing, the median price is in the neighborhood of $226,000.

It's now 1975 and you are standing by the water cooler, talking with someone who is considering making her first real estate investment. The market in your area went up last year, so the median price in your area is $30,000.

The discussion is about whether or not now is the time to buy. Should you wait a little longer or strike now? What if the market drops next year? Then it would have been better to wait and buy the property next year.

At the time of the discussion, whether you bought a property at $20,000 or $30,000 seemed like a big deal. If you were right and the property dropped 30% in value and you picked it up at the lower price, wouldn't that be a great deal?

The answer is maybe. It doesn't matter that much if you buy it at $30,000 or if you buy it at $20,000. Here's what matters: when you buy it, you can make positive cash flow from that investment and it is now in your portfolio. You own it and it is making money.

If you had been a real estate investor in 1975, like my grandparents were, how would that question appear today? With a median home value of $226,000 today, do you think it made any significant difference whether you bought the property for $20,000 or $30,000? The answer is no. For all practical purposes, they are the same. Both options made a lot of money, if you made the purchase. Neither option made money if you held off and never made the purchase because you were waiting for the market to bottom out.

You want property for cash flow and long-term growth in your investment portfolio. If you buy a good piece of property for the long haul, you will make a great profit. Long-term investing is the key. Speculators are thinking short-term.

What happens in the good and bad market years is the change in availability of good properties. In a super-hot market, all the speculators are scarfing up property so fast you can't get to them. Therefore, super-hot markets are not ideal for investors. But if you find a good deal, you should still take it.

The down markets will be slow enough for you to take the time to evaluate properties. There will be more positive cash flow properties when the prices are down and less when the prices are up. You need to find the good ones, either way.

MY EXPERIENCE IN A HOT MARKET

A hot market is moving fast. You put a property up for sale and three days later you have seven offers and half of them are more than you are asking. All the speculators are driving the prices up, which means more people want to jump on the bandwagon. This kind of market is hard for a busy professional to deal with.

Early in my real estate investing years, my father was retired from his job at the mill. He wasn't doing much so I thought it might be a great time to give him an opportunity. I had some spare cash and he had some spare time. It seemed like a great time for us to do some real estate fix-and-flip opportunities.

Don't confuse this with real estate investing. *Flipping properties is not investing; it's a job.* You buy a property, put some effort into finding a new buyer, maybe even do some fixing or updating, and sell the place for a profit. You earned the income over a few months for your labor and pay income tax on the profits. That is a job.

As a busy professional, you are already paid a good income by swapping your time and expertise for money. Flipping houses is not a good way for you to spend your time. You don't need a second job, you need long-term passive income from an investment.

In my case, my dad was not working and could use a job that paid well. I could provide the money and the property know-how and he could provide the labor. I figured we could split the profit from each flip. He would have something productive to do and we both could make a little money.

Unfortunately, we made this decision during a hot market. Real estate was selling fast. Prices were climbing fast. There were so many speculators in the market that it was too fast for me to do anything.

Since I was working full time, I had a time delay to evaluate a property. My realtor would call me with a great opportunity that just came on the market that morning. I was in surgery all day. I would swing by the property to look at it after work. If it looked like a good possibility, I would call the realtor and ask to set up a time to view the property, only to be told there were already five offers.

In a fast market, only those who can act immediately or are willing to buy property sight-unseen can get there fast enough.

We were beaten to the punch on everything we tried to buy. After a few months of that, we gave up as it seemed a waste of time to do the work without being able to buy a property.

Contrast that to a slow market: prices are not climbing so fast, so the speculators are not hunting for deals and you have time to evaluate a property. The realtor would call me, I could swing by after work, and we would be able to set up a walk-through the next day. Then I would have time to work the numbers and decide if it was a good deal for me. We could put in an offer and go through the negotiations and buy the property.

A slow market or a down market is so much nicer to work in. Since you will be cash-flow sensitive and not price sensitive, any market will do. But a slow market is easier to work with than a hot market.

MY SON'S EXPERIENCE IN A HOT MARKET

My son decided to buy his first rental property in 2016. Property was moving fairly quickly at the time. When he found something he liked, he asked me to look at it with him. He was looking for something he could get cheaply, so fixers were his target.

His plan was to buy it at a low price, fix it up, and rent it for the rest of his life, for long-term passive income. Unfortunately, lots of people were doing that at the time. He kept getting beat out on the good ones.

One day he found a promising prospect. It was a small two-bed, one-bath house. Their asking price was in the $60,000 range. Someone else's offer was already accepted when he put in his offer.

He kept the information on the place. We thought the asking price was a bargain. A few months later, he saw that same house go on the market again. It looked like the person who bought it started to fix it up and then just stopped to sell it again. Some of the work had been completed and some was still left to do.

Since he was already familiar with the property and already knew the new $70,000 asking price was still a bargain, he immediately put in an offer for the asking price, with all cash to close in a week. How can that offer be turned down?

Because of his quick action, he got the place. Over the next couple of months, he fixed it up with less than $10,000 and rented it out for $825 a month.

Most busy professionals—who are not contractors, realtors, or speculators—will not be able to act fast enough in a hot market, so don't worry about it. The market will slow down again soon and you will be able to get what you want then. Just be patient. This is a marathon, not a sprint.

THE WIN-WIN DEAL

As a real estate investor, what you are looking for is a win-win deal. You do not need to look for distressed properties, basement bargains, fixer-uppers, or any situation where you will be taking advantage of someone. A bargain would be a bonus but is not necessary. You can afford to pay a fair price for a good piece of property you will have for many years.

Fair prices on good property are always available in both hot and slow markets. People have lots of reasons for selling a property. You can give them a fair price for their property and still become wealthy buying real estate. Whatever price you pay today will seem like a bargain 20 years from now.

I have seen the following reasons for a property to be on the market:

- The owner wanted to retire and sail around the world.

- The owner had died and left the property to his kids, who wanted money, not property.

- The owner was providing a job for his daughter and she didn't want to be a property manager anymore, so he didn't need the property.

- The owner was the manager and was now too old to do it and wanted to convert his properties to cash with an interest income.

- The owner moved to another city and wanted her investment property to be close by, so was doing a 1031 exchange.

- A divorce was forcing the sale of the property.

- The owner retired and wanted to downsize to a smaller house.

- The owner got the property in exchange on another business deal and didn't want to keep it for himself.

- The property was owned in a partnership that was going to dissolve.

- The property had appreciated so much that the owner wanted to lock in the gains by selling now.

- The bank repossessed the property and they were not in the rental business.

As you can see, there are many reasons for a property to be on the market. These properties are not likely to be sold for bargain-basement prices. Since you don't need bargain-basement prices to invest in real estate, you are in luck.

The key to your success is that your investment must have a positive cash flow. I will talk in the next chapter about how to value your investment so you make the right purchases and always have a positive cash flow. Good properties that will create positive cash flow are always on the market.

Find a good realtor and teach them what you want. They see the properties coming on the market each day and will be on the lookout for what you want. When they find it, you can spend your time making an assessment of the property. You don't need to do all the legwork hunting down the winners. Let the realtor earn their money and find the good stuff for you.

BUYING AT THE MARKET PEAK

The most feared thing for the new real estate investor seems to be buying at the top of the market. Since you will not be trying to time the market and since you will be holding your property for decades, the peak of the market is not relevant to you. And for reasons unrelated to the price, it might not be the best time to buy.

Let me tell you about an experience I had with buying a property at the peak of the market in 2007. This would be an example of the worst-case scenario.

The 2000s were a time of incredible real estate profits. Everyone was making money in real estate. Because prices were rising at double digit rates each year, people were buying property sight unseen and reaping the profits. They would buy, hold for a year or two and sell for a profit. Those were good times for speculators. (You are not one of them!)

I had been doing well with real estate, and I wanted my family members to see the value of investing in real estate. I convinced some of them to partner with me so I could show them how.

We set up an LLC. We all contributed money for a down payment on a property and we each owned a percentage based on our contribution. Since I was already managing properties, I ran the LLC.

I owned the largest share of the company, so I had the most at risk, thus incentivizing the manager to do well.

We found a nine-unit apartment and bought it for $595,000 in 2007. We put $145,000 down and the seller carried the mortgage. The cash flow was positive, but the building needed some fixing. Our plan was to fix the property, keep it for five years, and then sell it for a handsome profit, assuming the hot market would continue. We paid current market price with a discount because it needed fixing. Both the seller and the partners thought we got a fair deal and it was a win-win transaction.

So we bought the place and started our adventure. A few months later, our worst fear was realized when the real estate market collapsed.

One of the partners panicked with the collapse and wanted out before it got worse. The rest of us were unwilling to sell the property for a loss. We bought that partner out at a discount based on the current depressed market value. Both sides of the deal were happy. He got out of what he perceived as a market meltdown before it hit bottom and we got a greater share of ownership of the property at a discount.

There were two errors in our investment plan:

The first was we were acting like speculators (hoping to sell in five years for a profit) and not investors. Thus we were dependent on the market for this to succeed. We got caught up in the real estate frenzy and wanted to take advantage of it. This approach did not follow the same successful plan I used for my other real estate investments, which was to hold them forever.

The second error was having a partnership in a fixer-upper. If I had made a mistake in calculating how much things would cost to fix, we might have needed a *capital call* (essentially asking the partners for more money) to get the job done. Capital calls are never good.

Over the first few years of this real estate meltdown, many properties were foreclosed on. Many real estate speculators lost their shirts. I know of one who committed suicide because his losses were so bad.

The market drop for apartments was not as bad as the drop for single-family homes. This is because apartment building values are based more on rental income and single-family home values are based more on emotion. The real market value on the assessor's books for our place fell to about the value of the mortgage. At that point, we would have lost our down payment money if we had sold.

I had an interesting conversation with the past owner of that apartment building, who held the mortgage. He had been bragging to me about how he gave his home back to the bank. He had bought a nice house on the river for about a million dollars and during the market fall, the value dropped to below the amount of the mortgage. So he gave it back to the bank and walked away.

He bragged about this poor financial decision as if he were a genius. It ruined his credit and he had to buy his next home in his son's name because he couldn't get a loan.

I was talking to him one day and hinted that we were going to give him the property back since the value had fallen to less than what we owed him. (He had told me that was the smart thing to do.) You should have seen the look on his face. He thought he made a killing selling right before the market drop and now he was going to get the property back and it might keep on dropping in value.

Funny how he didn't think that approach was OK when he was on the other end of the deal. We never actually thought of doing that to him, but it was fun to see him squirm with a little of his own medicine.

I believe in win-win deals and giving his property back to him would not be the right thing to do. It would have been a lose-lose deal. We would lose money selling it for a loss and he would get a property back he didn't want at a time he couldn't sell it.

Since we bought the property with a positive cash flow, and cash flow stayed positive throughout the market drop, we didn't lose anything. If you looked on paper, you could calculate a potential loss. But there was no actual loss since we didn't sell. We still collected rent and made our mortgage payments.

When the originally planned sell date came, the property was still worth less than we paid. We were not about to sell it for a loss when it was bringing in enough money to cover its expenses. We just held on and lengthened our five-year plan.

In 2018, the value of the property increased enough for us to sell it for a profit. We put the place on the market and ended up selling it for $779,500. This was 12 years after buying it on a five-year plan.

We bought it at the peak of the market, so it was the worst-case scenario for a speculative investment. One of the partners passed away during those 12 years and the estate was bought out by the rest of us.

I more than doubled my money and with the final accounting, my return was the equivalent of putting my investment in an interest-bearing account at 7.436% interest. So even in the worst case, the investment turned out well because we were willing to ride out the market changes.

Over the long haul, the market changes that are happening at the time you purchase a property will have little effect on your overall investment return. It is the appreciation over a long period of time that will make up for the little fluctuations.

The market will always go up and down. You will always be wondering where it will go next. The debate at the water cooler will continue. Are we at the peak or trough of the current swing? And in the long run, it is all irrelevant. For the real estate investor, these issues don't matter. Only the short-term speculator will be worried about the current market conditions.

"Don't wait to buy land.
Buy land and wait."

— Will Rogers

WHY PEOPLE LOSE IN A REAL ESTATE CRASH

Not everyone came out OK from the 2008 market crash. I told you of one suicide. Many people went bankrupt and out of business. Many properties were given back to the bank. The entire banking system was revamped. But for me, nothing happened of consequence.

What was the difference between all of those who lost money, and those who did not?

> ## "We don't have to be smarter than the rest. We have to be more disciplined than the rest."
>
> ## — Warren Buffett

Discipline is a key word in real estate investing. You need to set a plan in motion that will work even in bad times. If your plan will only work if next year is a good year, you are doomed to future failure.

Most of the people who lost money in the real estate bust were doing things they should not have done. They did things that were not safe financially, like the following:

- They bought more house than they could afford, stretching the payments to the max.
- They bought a home based on both wage earners' salaries. Then something happened to one of the salaries.
- They bought more units than they could handle.
- They borrowed more money than the property could support.
- They had an adjustable rate mortgage.
- They had a balloon payment in the mortgage.
- Their system was dependent on selling property every year.

Many other things like those listed above can put you at too much risk.

Notice that zero money down is not on the list. Buying property with no money down is not inherently risky. If the value of the property drops, it doesn't make any difference—just like the investment I made with my partners was not hurt by the drop in value of the property. As long as you don't have to sell, make a balloon payment, or have an adjustable rate mortgage, it doesn't matter how much you put down on an investment property.

The least risky investment for you is no money down. If you lost the property, you don't lose anything. You have nothing invested. That's why the bank wants you to make a big down payment. It is not to lessen the risk for you. It is to lessen the risk to the lender. The more skin you have in the game, the less likely you will be to default on the loan.

The way to avoid getting burned by a downturn in the market is to always buy your investments assuming there will be a downturn in the market. Always make the investment a safe one when you buy it. This is the reasoning behind this old saying:

You make your money in real estate when you buy, not when you sell.

There are some catastrophes that no one can plan for. When one of these happen, you are likely to lose no matter how well you prepared. These include a forest fire wiping out the entire town, a hurricane washing away your property and those around you, the main employer of the area going out of business, or being located in a town that gets bypassed by a new highway, which happened all along Route 66.

There is no way you can plan for these events. Bad things can happen with any investment you make. They are not unique to real estate. You can only plan for the things that are likely to happen.

If you always buy with safe terms, you are unlikely to get burned by market turns. Please read this chapter every year so you don't fall into becoming a real estate speculator and instead continue to be a real estate investor.

When walking through the woods, it's not a falling tree you need to worry about. It's the small root on the trail you need to watch out for.

Chapter 5

PREPARATION FOR BUYING INVESTMENT REAL ESTATE

Part of your education in preparing for buying investment real estate is understanding how investing is different from purchasing your family home and learning the strategies you need to be successful. This means dispelling myths about what makes an investment risky and understanding the elements you need to evaluate to feel secure.

UNDERSTANDING RISK

Risk in real estate investing is grossly misunderstood. There is risk in everything you do. You take a risk when you drive to work, when you ride a bicycle, when you get married, *and* when you invest in real estate. The key is to understand the risks and rewards, and keep the two in balance.

When we go on a bicycle ride, we do things to lessen the risk: ride on the correct side of the street, wear a helmet, put on gloves, use a headlight and tail light, watch for traffic, and don't do stupid things while yelling, "Watch this!"

The same is true with real estate investing, and there are things you can do to lessen the risk.

THE MORTGAGE

Some people believe no-money-down real estate investing is risky and to make it safe, one needs a 20% down payment. This is false security for the investor. In reality there is very little difference between 100% financed and 80% financed. If the goal is to hold the property for a long time and reap the cash flow rewards, then those two options essentially have the same risk. The hype about making a bigger down payment is to lessen the risk to the lender, not to lessen the risk to you.

The risk doesn't really drop until the mortgage is paid off. Yes, it is true that the lower the mortgage, the smaller the risk of a loan default, but it is not true that a slightly lower mortgage poses a significantly different risk. With a mortgage versus without a mortgage is a big jump in risk. Financing with a 100% mortgage versus an 80% mortgage is a very small difference in risk.

The way to lessen the risk of the mortgage is to evaluate the property and buy the right one with the right terms. As long as the cash flow is positive, the size of the mortgage doesn't matter. The size of the mortgage only comes into play when you sell. And as a real estate investor, I think you should plan on holding the property for a long time.

> ## "Our favorite holding period is forever."
> ## — Warren Buffet

Consider these key things about a mortgage:

- Make sure the cash flow will support the payments with room to spare.
- Avoid adjustable rate mortgages.
- Avoid balloon payments with short holding periods. Ten years is good, one year is risky.

Keeping those things in mind will keep the mortgage risk at bay.

CAREFULLY EVALUATE CASH FLOW BEFORE MAKING THE OFFER

The next risk-minimizing concept is to only invest in properties with a positive cash flow. This is the long-term best investing method for real estate.

> ## Cash flow is king.

Many methods have been published for evaluating investment real estate opportunities, and they have value as screening tools and sometimes as negotiating tools—I'll discuss this in greater detail later.

But the bottom-line question is whether or not the property will create positive cash flow. Your reason for investing is to create passive income. No positive cash flow, no passive income. I dedicate an entire chapter to a discussion of my methods for evaluating cash flow. For now, understand that it's the most important factor.

Bare land does not create a positive cash flow. It has a carrying cost as well. Never buy bare land as an investment. The only two times I ever bought bare land were when I had a very specific purpose for the purchase. One was to build a house and the other was to build an office building. Another purpose for bare land might be as a buffer, such as buying the lot next to your house so no one builds on it. But keep in mind that is not an investment. It is a luxury purchase.

I was approached once to join a partnership to buy some land in a growing area. "It will be a great investment someday," was how it was presented. I didn't bite. That was over 20 years ago and they still haven't developed the property. That's a lot of time to not make any cash flow on an investment. There has been some appreciation during that time, but they have been paying property taxes and mowing fees to hold that property, waiting for a sale.

The safe move is to buy a property that can be rented immediately. I like to buy apartments and close on the last day of the month. Then the next day, I'm collecting rent. I make money on the property from day one. Building your own apartment complex sounds nice, but there is a long period of no income during construction.

"After buying an investment property, the value of the property has no effect on my day-to-day life. It's all about the cash flow."

— Brian Fawcett

VALUE

The third way you can minimize the risk is to get value for the purchase. I will show you later how to make a good evaluation of a property. Don't pay more than you feel the property is worth at today's fair market value. Then if some catastrophe happens in your life, you can sell it for what it's worth.

I made this mistake once. I got caught up in a property that sounded good. It was in the right neighborhood for me and matched well with the other properties I owned. The problem was it had a negative cash flow and I thought the price was a bit too high.

The price and terms of the property, after I worked out the value, did not make any money each month. I let the realtor talk me into buying a property I should have passed on, even though it seemed like a nice property.

The property had a $17,739 NOI and a mortgage payment of $24,224 for a negative cash flow of $6,485 per year. How did I justify this move to myself? Since $4,500 of the mortgage payment went to principal each year, which is equity but not cash flow and would be considered profit to me, I was only losing $1,985 a year. It was financed 100% and I knew I would be paying down some of that mortgage and then the cash flow would become positive again—but that cash flow remained negative for several years. I could have put in a down payment and lowered the mortgage payments to make it a positive cash flow, but I didn't. It was a bad investment. Don't repeat my mistake.

DECIDE WHAT TYPE OF REAL ESTATE YOU WANT

There are many different types of investment real estate. I would suggest you pick one type and stick to it until you become comfortable and have good systems in place. (More about systems later.) Then, if you want to branch out into another type of investment real estate, you can learn the nuances of that second type.

SINGLE-FAMILY HOMES

The easiest type of real estate investment to start with is the single-family home. You have probably lived in one and have probably already purchased one, although not for investment purposes.

Even this category has several subcategories to deal with: traditional houses, mobile homes, condominiums, small snowbirding mobile homes called park models, vacation homes, manufactured homes, and single-apartment units in big cities.

Each of these subcategories have their own pluses and minuses. The advantages of single units are the low cost and ease of purchase. Here are some of the disadvantages: no economies of scale, the properties tend to be spread out, and when they are vacant, it has a 100% vacancy rate.

I have never owned a single-family home as a rental, but this is how my grandparents made their money in real estate. My son has also begun in this area, as have many others.

MULTIFAMILY HOMES (APARTMENTS)

This is my favorite type of real estate investment. This is commonly called an apartment building. They come in all sizes: duplex, triplex, fourplex, eight-unit, 30-unit, 250-unit, and more.

THE DOCTORS GUIDE TO REAL ESTATE INVESTING FOR BUSY PROFESSIONALS

For some people these can be intimidating, but they shouldn't be. They are easier to take care of and more profitable than owning several single-family homes.

The advantages of these are the economies of scale:

- Fewer roofs per unit

- Only one garbage can (dumpster)

- All of them are at the same location so two units can have repairs done in the same trip

- All the appliances can be the same so fewer spare parts are needed

- The cost per unit is lower

Contrary to popular belief, it is actually easier to manage a multifamily unit than several single-family homes.

The more units there are in a building, the lower the purchase price per door. Buying a rental for half the price and renting it out for the same monthly rent as the person who paid double for the rental is very rewarding. For example, my fourplex cost me more than $100,000 per unit to buy, but my 31-unit apartment only cost $37,000 per unit to buy. Each of the units rents for about the same. So the 31-unit building makes much more profit per unit than the smaller one.

I think the best break point is at about eight units. In the future, I think I will stick to apartment complexes that are eight units or bigger, if I ever get back into the buying mode. (I already have enough to take care of my family financially for the rest of our lives.)

The disadvantages of multifamily units are the overall purchase price is higher and the lending costs are higher—if it has five or more units, it falls into the commercial real estate domain. Commercial real estate has higher interest rates and higher appraisal costs.

Most of the real estate income I generate is from this category.

COMMERCIAL BUILDINGS

This one is the next level of scary for the new investor. These would be places for businesses to rent. Many businesses do not own their building. As a new business starts, they usually are short on capital. Because of this, they tend to rent a building and only if they become very successful do they buy a building.

Most new businesses fail in the first few years. That means the commercial building becomes vacant. Vacancies in commercial buildings tend to last for a longer time than vacancies in residential property. Many more people want a place to live than there are businesses needing a building to rent.

Some of the best commercial rentals to own are rented by franchises. Most people don't realize that many fast food joints do not own the building they are in. Owning the building that houses a very successful franchise, like a Dairy Queen or a Pizza Hut, can make for a very stable, low vacancy rate investment. The U.S. Postal service also makes for a very steady and stable tenant.

I have owned a few commercial buildings over the years and today I still own two of them, each in a partnership. One is doing very well. It houses a single business that uses the entire building. If they go out of business, it could stand vacant for a long time. Fortunately the mortgage is paid off now and the tenant business is doing well.

The other one houses many different businesses, but it has not produced much in the way of income due to turnovers and vacancies.

I have some friends who own commercial buildings with triple-net leases and are very happy with the arrangements. A triple-net lease means the tenant will be paying general maintenance costs, property taxes, and building insurance, in addition to the rent.

VACATION RENTALS

This is an interesting way to enter the real estate business. Many people who do this start with their own vacation home and begin to rent it out. After they realize they are making money on the deal, they buy more rentals.

This can be a dicey deal. There are no stable tenants. If the economy drops, vacationing is one of the first things people cut back on. It can be fun to own a personal vacation spot and make a little money on the side, but as a business, it is riskier.

I do not own any vacation rentals but I have friends who do.

Each of these investment categories is different. They have different contracting and vacancy possibilities. The skill needed to run each of them is also different. Pick your favorite and concentrate on doing it well and learn everything you need to know to be successful.

The easiest, and my favorite, is the small apartment buildings, about 8 to 12 units in size. These have some economies of scale and are still small enough for the beginning investor to buy. There are also other categories such as storage units, cell towers, farmland, timber, Christmas tree farms, and others.

FIND A GOOD REALTOR

Having a good realtor working on your behalf is the best way for you to find real estate. You don't have the time to do the research and chase down leads. The realtor will do it full time and you don't even have to pay them!

The key is to find a good one and teach her your purchase criteria. If you don't train her well, she will bring everything to you, hoping to get a sale.

I found a great realtor who used to be a real estate investor himself. I showed him exactly what I wanted. There was a little breaking-in period and then he got the picture. After that, he brought about two properties to my attention each year. I would evaluate them, and I bought about a third of what he showed me.

Here is the criteria I asked the realtor to use for screening to find me a "plum" property:

- Multifamily complex
- Positive cash flow using my formula (I will show you this later)
- Cash flow is still positive if 100% financing is used
- Mortgage of less than 25% of the price so owner financing might be possible
- Constructed after 1980 when lead paint was no longer used
- Few current vacancies
- Minimal deferred maintenance
- Within a 20-minute drive from my home

Some realtors are just trying to make a buck and don't really know much about real estate. Others are very good at what they do and will be a great help to you.

I had one realtor contact me with a promising apartment. I looked it over and did not make an offer. I then described to him what I wanted, my plum property using the above list. I asked him to only call me if he found a plum.

He called me every day with another "plum," except it wasn't. Each time I explained to him why it was not a plum and he just didn't get it. He could not understand how to evaluate an investment property. A pretty building at a good price in a good location is not necessarily a good investment property. If it doesn't meet your needs, pass it by and let someone else buy it. I asked him to stop calling me.

Another realtor called me about a property right across the street from one I already owned. I looked at it and was interested. I told her to set up a meeting for me to talk with the seller. She called me back and said she talked to the seller and he was not interested in carrying the mortgage.

This realtor obviously did not do what I asked. I did not ask her to ask the seller if he would carry the mortgage, I asked her to set up a meeting for me to talk with the seller. She presumed and did what she wanted. If the realtor can't follow your instructions, you need to find a better realtor.

Once you find a good realtor and train them for what you want, you will be very happy with the results. They will call you when something comes on the market fitting your specifications. Then you don't have to go looking on your own. This is a tremendous time-saver.

HOW TO BUY "FOR SALE BY OWNER" PROPERTY

Of note, most realtors will not look at properties that are *for sale by owner*, as the owner will not be paying their commission. Those are often the plums you are looking for. You have two choices with this.

First, you can tell the realtor you will give them a 2-3% commission on any *for sale by owner* property they bring you. That is the commission they would have received anyway as the buyer's realtor—the total sales commission typically runs 5-6% and is split by the selling and buying realtors. You can use a realtor to represent you in that sale. *Do not sign a contract stating you will pay them for anything you buy,* whether you use them or not. Only agree to pay them if they find it for you.

I had a realtor try this on me when we were looking for a site to build a home, before we started real estate investing. I had been looking at *for sale by owner* stuff as well as other properties. I kept calling him and asking him to check on a property for me. Eventually he asked me to sign a contract giving him a commission for anything I bought, even if he didn't get involved. I pointed out to him that I found about half of the properties we were considering and brought them to the table myself. And I stopped using that realtor.

Second, you can let the realtor search the properties on the MLS (Multiple Listing Service), and you can search *for sale by owner* material. This means you will be looking in the newspaper, on the internet, and at the signs you might drive by that say *for sale by owner.*

For sale by owner is how I conducted my recent apartment sale. I advertised it in the local newspaper, the newspaper in the next town, and on Craigslist. I did not put a sign out in front of the building. I was contacted by 10 interested buyers over about two months and sold the property to one of them.

The person who bought the property did not feel comfortable without a realtor on her side. She hired a realtor to represent her and she paid his commission. We were all happy with the deal.

Chapter 6

SCREENING PROPERTY INVESTMENTS

Once you find a property you are interested in buying, you must crunch the numbers to be sure it will be profitable. I have seen several properties that looked good on drive-by but did not look good on paper. Often this is because the owner wants too much money for the property.

To become a real estate investor, profit is the key. Every property must be fully evaluated for its profit potential. If it will not make a profit (cash flow), keep looking. Do not feel bad about passing on a property and don't let the realtor talk you out of your decision. No matter how nice the place seems, the goal is to make a profit. And as a busy professional, the goal is not a quick profit, but a long-term profit. Pencil out every property to be sure it will work. There are several value methods for doing this, and I suggest you use most of them as screening and negotiating methods only. They give you good information but may not show you the complete picture.

In the next chapter, I'll describe how to truly evaluate the investment potential of a property, using what I consider to be the gold standard: cash flow. I've mentioned the term before, and that chapter will show you how to calculate the potential cash flow of an investment property.

CHECK THE SOURCE OF ADVICE

I'm sure you are already reading up on how to invest in real estate, but be careful about believing everything you read. I have seen many people write about how to evaluate properties. Often, they do not know what they are talking about. Much of what you find on the internet is written by "content writers." These are people who do a little research into something and write about it. They don't actually know about the topic. They make their living by writing about "stuff"—any topic will do.

I didn't realize how prevalent this was until I started my blog, Prescription for Financial Success. Once I became better known, people began to come out of the woodwork asking to write guest posts for my blog. They were usually "content writers" and guaranteed they would put together something that would appeal to my audience.

SCREENING PROPERTY INVESTMENTS

When I evaluated what they sent, I could tell that they did not know anything about the topic. They simply looked on the internet at what other "content writers" had published and rearranged it for me. It often had bad advice or advice that was not pertinent to my audience.

Be careful about getting this type of advice. A lot of it is wrong. An example is the 1% rule. This rule states that a rental unit should be profitable if the monthly rent will be at least 1% of the purchase price. For example, if the price is $200,000, the 1% rule means it will be a good rental property if you can rent it for at least $2,000 a month.

A SCREENING TOOL IS NOT A DECISION-MAKING TOOL

But the 1% rule is only a screening tool to help you sort through a lot of properties to find which ones might work. It is not a tool for determining if the particular property is a good investment. I see many people writing about this rule as a way for them to decide if they will buy a property. They go as far as to say, "Don't buy that property because it doesn't meet the 1% rule." That is not what the rule is for. It is only a screening tool.

If a property rents for way under 1% of the purchase price, it is less likely to be a good investment but still could be. If a property rents for way over 1%, it is more likely to be a good investment but still might not be. But the 1% rule cannot tell you if a specific property is or is not a good investment. Do not use a screening tool as a decision-maker.

In medicine, we use a lot of screening tools. One of them is the hemoccult card check of your stool as a screen for colon cancer. This test is a small card that detects the presence of hemoglobin (blood) in the stool. Cancer can leak blood and make the test positive. If the test is positive, it means you have some hemo-globin in your stool and you should have a closer look to see if you might have cancer. A positive test does not mean you have colon cancer—there are other causes for blood in stool. It only means your doctor should take a closer look.

That closer look is the actual test to see if the cancer is there: a colonoscopy. If the colonoscopy is clear, you do not have colon cancer, no matter what the screening test showed. If the colonoscopy finds cancer, then you need surgery. Why do we do the screening test? Because it is cheaper and easier than the definitive test. It's a way to identify the patients who need the bigger, more time-consuming and expensive testing.

No doctor will advise surgery to take out part of your colon because the screening test was positive. And no real estate in-vestor should buy a property because it passed the 1% rule. The screening test is not a decision-maker. It is only a reason to take a closer look at something. If you see someone giving advice to definitively act on a screening test, keep looking for better advice.

SETTING THE PRICE

Since you will have to make a real offer on a property if you want to buy it, you will need to come up with a way to set your offer price. There are several ways to do this. The bottom line is this: any price you set must result in positive cash flow or it will not be a good investment.

> ## The offer price must result in positive cash flow or it will not be a good investment.

It always comes back to cash flow. The reason I will go over the different ways to value the property is so you will be able to back up the price you plan to offer. I will cover some different ways to value property, and then will go over the only one that counts: *cash flow.*

The cash flow calculation is the most important section of this book and you will come back to it every time you get ready to buy a property, as you work to assess its value by penciling out the figures. If you make a mistake here, it will be costly. You make your money when you buy the property. If the property will not make you money, don't buy it.

This is not a time to let your emotions get in the way. Real estate does not have a set market price. There is no Kelly Blue Book to set the price. It is more of an art and a negotiation. So the more you understand your local market, the better you will be at finding a good price. The more you can back up your number, the more likely you will be to get your price.

COMPARISONS

This is also known as *comps* in the real estate world. This is a way of looking at your possible investment property in light of how similar properties have been valued.

This is a great place to utilize your realtor. They can do this work for you. It's pretty easy to do this with single-family homes, as usually many have sold recently. It is harder for multifamily units and commercial buildings because sales are fewer.

An important point is to look at the recent *selling* prices, not the listing prices. It is very easy to look at Zillow and see what houses are listed for, or what Zillow thinks they are worth. It is also easy to look at the county tax assessor information and get what the assessor thinks it is worth.

But those sources of information are all guesses. You want to know what a *buyer* thinks it's worth. For that, you need to look at recent sales information. Your realtor has easy access to that info and can quickly get you some comps. You can also look at this on Zillow if you don't look at the properties for sale, but instead look at the properties that recently sold.

It is also important that you are comparing apples to apples. With single-family homes, you rarely can find an exact copy of the home in question to compare. So you are looking for something similar—same number of beds and baths, similar year built, similar neighborhood, and similar size.

This mostly gives you an idea if the seller is asking a reasonable price for the property. It will not tell you if it is a good investment.

When it comes to multifamily and commercial properties, the comps will be harder to come by. When I was getting ready to sell my nine-plex in 2018, there were no comps in the area to look at.

I had to expand my search to other apartments throughout the state. But there was quite a difference in asking price for an apartment in a town of 10,000 people and a city of 500,000 people. Prices were very different throughout the state. But it still gave me an idea of what things were selling for.

The price is figured differently for a single-family home than for a multifamily home. The best benchmark to use is *price per unit.*

If a 10-unit apartment sells for $1,000,000, then the comp is $100,000 per unit. Since you will be renting it out per unit, price it that way in your comps for easier comparisons across different-sized apartment complexes.

CAPITALIZATION RATE (CAP RATE)

This is another commonly used method to establish the value of an investment property. In order to get this number, you need a lot more information about the property. With multi-family units, the cap rate is often listed in the sales offer. **Don't take the number they give you at face value.** Calculate your own cap rate.

To figure the cap rate, you must know the net operating income (NOI). The seller should give you their income and expenses so you can calculate this. First, you take a year's worth of actual income from all sources. That figure will already have the vacancy rate built into it. This includes such things as the quarters from the laundry machines.

Then subtract the year's total expenses. All expenses should be included except for debt service (mortgage payment) and depreciation. This includes property taxes, insurance, homeowners association fees, advertising, water, sewer, garbage, electricity, gas, oil, yard care, accounting, management, and repairs.

So if the rental and laundry income was $100,000 last year and the total expenses were $40,000, then the net operating income is $60,000. That is the amount of money the property makes when it is fully owned with no mortgage.

Income – Expenses (excluding mortgage) = NOI

The cap rate is the rate of return the property would generate if you purchased it with cash—a true evaluation of the property as an investment. This is usually done on an annual basis. To get this figure, simply divide the NOI by the purchase price. Note, this does not take mortgage interest rates, appreciation, or closing costs into account—or the tax advantages it represents (more on taxes later).

NOI/Purchase Price = Cap Rate

EXAMPLE CAP RATE CALCULATION

Let's use a property that can be purchased for $700,000 cash as an example. First you must determine the NOI. The rental income is $100,000 per year. The expenses of the property are $40,000 per year. Income - expenses would be $100,000 - $40,000 = $60,000 NOI.

The cap rate is NOI/purchase price which is $60,000/$700,000 = 0.0857. Multiplying this figure by 100 converts it to a percentage. So, 0.0857 x 100 = 8.57% cap rate.

This property would be expected to return 8.57% on the money invested in an all-cash deal. To get an equivalent deal, the money would need to be invested in a bank account or other investment that would return 8.57%.

This number becomes very useful when considering how the property will be financed. If the current interest rate for commercial loans is 8.57% or less, the property could be financed 100% and it would break even or make money. If the current interest rate is greater than this on mortgages, then the down payment would need to increase to a point where the property is making more than the financing costs.

CAP RATE VERSUS MORTGAGE RATE BENCHMARK

In general, you should not consider buying any property with a cap rate less than the going rate for the mortgage interest you can obtain. This becomes another benchmark to decide if the investment might be worth it.

When the current mortgage rate is at 5%, then a 6% cap rate is reasonable. When I purchased my first property, the current mortgage rate was 8%. In order for the property to work, it would need to have a cap rate of at least 8%. My first year NOI was $110,599. The purchase price was $1,150,000. So my cap rate was 110,599/1,150,000 = 0.0962. Multiplying that by 100 gives a Cap Rate of 9.62%. Since the apartment returns 9.6% and I can get financing for 8%, it should be a good buy at 100% financing.

Cap Rate > Mortgage Interest Rate

This is not a hard-and-fast rule. So even if the current interest rate is 8%, a property can still be a good investment for you if it has a cap rate of 6%—if it was purchased with all cash. When you buy with all cash, the cap rate doesn't really matter since you are not paying interest on financing. It is still a benchmark for comparison to other properties. There could be a good reason why you would be fine with getting a 6% return on your investment. Especially when you consider it will be partly tax-free and market appreciation will add even more to the overall return.

Cap rate can be used in reverse to get the maximum amount you could offer. For example, let's say I only want to buy properties with a cap rate of 8% or better. Since the property in the previous example has an NOI of $60,000, I can divide 60,000 by the 0.08 cap rate I want for a return, and I get $750,000. That would mean my maximum offer should not exceed $750,000.

If the asking price was $725,000, I can pay the asking price with confidence since it is less than my maximum price.

Maximum Purchase Price = NOI/Desired Cap Rate

Because the cap rate is based on the NOI, it can be manipulated. For example, my first purchase had below-market rent rates charged to the tenants. If it had an NOI of $60,000 and the moment I took over I increased the rent by $25 per month to each tenant, I would have dramatically changed the cap rate. With 31 tenants, the NOI just went up by $9,300 a year. Using an 8% cap rate, that increase in NOI increased the value of the property by $9,300/0.08 = $116,250. Put another way, the rent increase changes the NOI to $69,300 and, with the purchase price of $750,000, the cap rate went up to 9.24% ($69,300/$750,000 = 0.0924 x 100 = 9.24%) from the 8.57% we calculated before the rent increase.

Therefore, if the cap rate was a little low for me at the time of purchase, but I knew I could raise the rent right away, I could go ahead with the deal knowing it would be better in a few months.

Also keep in mind the numbers you have to work with to calculate NOI were supplied by the current owner. For this reason, I always ask to see the last two years' tax returns on the property. Then I can see if the numbers the owner gave me match the numbers the owner told the government. If they do not match, I find out why. Every seller should be willing to provide this information during escrow. If it is not provided, ask for it and *do not even consider buying the property* if the seller will not supply this information.

This information will either be found on the owner's schedule E tax form or the property's tax returns.

I once had an owner tell me the coin-operated laundry room made $5,000 a year. The tax forms stated the laundry made only $2,000 a year. When I asked him why the difference, he told me since it was all cash, he didn't tell the IRS about the extra $3,000.

So now I know the owner I'm dealing with is a liar and a thief and if he would cheat the IRS, when the consequences could include jail, then he would cheat me, when the consequences are less. When this happens to you, be very careful about each step dealing with this seller. Also, use the lower number when you calculate the property value because you already know he is bending the truth, and he could be bending the truth about the $5,000 he says the laundry makes each year. Maybe it really makes the $2,000 a year figure he gave to the IRS but he wants you to think it makes more to raise the purchase price. Always calculate things yourself and look over all the numbers to see that they make sense.

At one point, I was talking with an owner who was selling a business stated to earn $40,000 per year in profit.

When I asked him, "So, a guy could make a living off this business?" He balked at that. On further inquiry, what he meant to say was there was $40,000 available to pay for *all* labor. So if the new owner did all the labor, they would make $40,000. But as I looked around the business, I could see three employees working and none of them were the owner. I also didn't see how the business could run with less than three employees.

It turned out the business had never made any profit for the owner. In fact, it had lost about $100,000 per year since it opened its doors. When I asked why he advertised it with a $40,000 profit, he said this: "If I had advertised it lost money every year, no one would even look at it."

He's right. No one wants to buy an investment that is guaranteed to lose money. If I had not looked into the numbers myself and just went off what the owner presented, I could have made a big mistake.

Cap rate is not a make-or-break number. Use it to compare the property to other property investments and to mortgage costs. Keep it in context.

APPRAISALS

This is the most common way a bank will set the value of a property. They will make you hire someone who specializes in setting the value of property and let them confirm the purchase price is appropriate.

For a single-family home, an appraisal might cost you $400. The most common method the appraiser will use is comparisons to similar properties, and they will also look at what it would cost to replace the home.

For a commercial property, which includes all multifamily properties with five or more units, the cost of an appraisal is more like $5,000.

The appraiser will use the income and expenses of the property to set the value, just as I described for the cap rate calculation. The property will be treated more like a business, to determine the size of the loan the property can handle and how much the bank is willing to loan.

You make an offer on the property, then the appraiser will come in and declare if the property is worth the offer. If the appraisal comes in under that value, it doesn't mean the bank won't loan money on the property. It simply changes the amount the bank will finance.

Let's say the offer on a property is $500,000 and the bank will loan 70% of the appraised value. That would mean I have to come up with $150,000 for the down payment and the bank will cover the $350,000 left with a mortgage.

Then the appraisal is done and comes in at a value of $450,000. The bank only agreed to lend me 70% of the property value, which is now lower than the agreed-upon purchase price. The bank will only loan 70% of the appraised value, which now computes to $315,000, not the originally $350,000.

Since the offer is $500,000 and the bank will only loan $315,000, I can still do the deal but will now need a down payment of $185,000 to move forward.

As an additional option, I could use the lower appraisal value to get the seller to agree to a lower purchase price.

This is a reason to have loan information as a contingency in the offer. If the loan will not come through at $350,000, then I have a way to back out of the deal if I want. You might word this like, "This offer is contingent on attaining good terms on a mortgage of at least $350,000."

If the bank will not loan the $350,000, then the contingency is not met and you can walk away from the deal and get your earnest money back.

Most of my property purchases were done without using a bank and I didn't even bother getting a formal appraisal done, as it was a waste of money for me. It is really only used to protect the bank, so they will require it. Since I will be holding the property for a long time and the property has a positive cash flow, the appraised value doesn't matter to me. In essence, I did the appraisal myself and saved $5,000.

Chapter 7

CASH FLOW METHOD OF EVALUATING REAL ESTATE INVESTMENTS—THE GOLD STANDARD

The property evaluation methods listed in the previous chapter are only good to use as negotiating tools to get the price you want. Cash flow is the only method I use to determine the value of the property to me and it is my decision-making tool.

Cash flow is how I determine the price I'm willing to pay. It is the only way to fully evaluate the property as an investment, and it will take some of your time to compute. It also takes into consideration how the property is financed—which none of the other methods care about, but you certainly should.

When I buy an investment property, the idea is to make money. That's the definition of an investment: a place to put your money so it will make you more money. There are two ways real estate makes money. One is appreciation, which I can't predict well, and the other is cash flow, which is much more predictable.

In order for you to compute the cash flow, you will need two pieces of information already discussed: income and expenses, which make up the NOI. The final piece of information is the financing terms, which I cover in the next chapter.

It is unlikely you will be buying your investment property with all cash. You will need to get a loan or mortgage on the property. It is very important that the money coming from the property, the NOI, can fully cover the mortgage payments.

This is the key to why it is OK to borrow money to make a real estate investment but not to buy a car. When you borrow to buy a car, you will personally need to earn the money to make those payments, and that means the car payments take away from your available cash flow. A car loan creates a negative cash flow.

With an investment property mortgage, the property is responsible for earning the money to make the payments. You can then put the leftovers in your pocket: a positive cash flow. So a property investment loan puts money into your pocket and the car loan takes money out of your pocket.

The cash flow calculations determine if you will have an investment that puts money into your pocket or takes money out.

Let's go over this important step in detail. We will do this as if you are purchasing a multi-family unit, but the exercise is the same no matter what you are buying.

CASH FLOW ANALYSIS FORM

Put all the numbers in the following form as a yearly total. Following the form is a description of each number you will need.

CASH FLOW ANALYSIS

Gross Income
    Scheduled Rent   _____
    Estimated Laundry   _____
    Other Income   _____
Estimated Income   _____
    Less Vacancy Allowance   _____
Estimated Gross Income   _____

Expenses
    Accounting & Legal   _____
    Advertising   _____
    Business Expense   _____
    Electricity   _____
    Eviction   _____
    Garbage   _____
    Gas   _____
    Groundskeeping   _____
    Insurance   _____
    Licenses   _____
    Management   _____
    Miscellaneous   _____
    Office Supplies & Postage   _____
    Pest Control   _____
    Pool Upkeep   _____
    Property Taxes   _____
    Repair & Maintenance   _____
    Snow Removal   _____
    HOA Fees   _____
    Telephone   _____
    Water & Sewer   _____
Total Expenses   _____

Net Operating Income   _____

Debt Service
    1st Mortgage   _____
    2nd Mortgage   _____
    3rd Mortgage   _____
Total Debt Service   _____

Cash Flow   _____

GROSS INCOME

The first thing to look at is the gross income. The seller should provide a *rent roll,* which is a list of every unit, its number of bedrooms and baths, and current rent for the unit. After entering escrow with a completed sales agreement, the seller will provide a copy of every tenant contract and you can compare the rent roll with the contracted rents. Also, when you get a chance, you can ask each tenant what they are paying to be sure it matches the rent roll you received.

You will sometimes encounter a seller who presents the property's income at market rates—what you could rent the units for instead of what the tenants are actually paying. This is done in order to boost the perceived value of the property. It is important that all your calculations are made off of the *actual rent received* and not potential rent received.

This very thing hurt the seller of the 31-unit complex I purchased. He had the actual rents well under market value. He would have liked to price his apartment at what it would bring in if everyone paid market value. Unfortunately for him, he had to use the actual rents. That was to my favor.

Once you know the scheduled rent, an allowance needs to be made for vacancies. Every place will have some vacancy. If someone moves out, there will be a few days required for the unit to be cleaned, repaired, and ready to rent to the next tenant. A period of time is also needed to qualify the next tenant.

This gap in rent collection is called vacancy. This is a big expense and you must get an accurate assessment of its cost. There are two ways to determine vacancy rate. The first is to ask around and see what other investors are experiencing for vacancy. Often a local rental owners association can provide a number for the current vacancy rate in the area.

The second is to use the seller's schedule E from the last two years' tax returns to see how actual collections compared to scheduled collections.

Once you have a number for estimated vacancy, then you can adjust your scheduled rents down by that figure. For example, if the vacancy rate runs about 5% in the area, which is about 18 days per year per unit, then you can multiply the scheduled rent by 0.05 to get the expected income loss due to vacancy for each year. This would be subtracted from the scheduled rent. (This figure can also be found by multiplying the scheduled rent by 0.95 to get the rental income adjusted for vacancy.)

Next you need to add in all the ancillary income from the property. This could include the laundry room, vending machines, covered parking fees, garage rental, and any other moneys the property brings in.

Adding up the scheduled rent, adjusted for vacancies and other income, will give you the total estimated gross income of the property. Compare this number to what the seller has presented as the gross income and discuss with the seller any discrepancies you find. Sellers often list the scheduled rent, without vacancies, as the property income to boost the figure. Watch out for that practice.

If the scheduled rent is below market value, and you know you will be raising the rent after you acquire the property, you should consider using those new numbers in your calculations. For example, if you bought my 31-unit complex and were planning on raising the rent by $25 per unit, that would raise your gross income by $9,300 per year. That is 31 units x $25 a month x 12 Months = $9,300. This will give you a more accurate assessment of how the property will perform. If you want to be conservative, leave the numbers at the pre-rent-increase value.

EXPENSES

Next you need to calculate the estimated expenses, not including financing. Usually the seller will not list all the expenses in the prospectus. They tend to leave off a few things, which makes the value of the property seem higher. You need to be sure to add all the expenses you will encounter so your figures are as close as possible to reality. The most common expense sellers leave off is management costs. If you will use a management company, you must include the expense.

Getting a full understanding of the expenses is the most important part of the pre-purchase evaluation. For this reason, you want some proof to back up the seller's claims and your calculations. So every offer must include the seller providing you either the tax returns for the property, if it has its own return, or their schedule E from their last two personal tax returns.

The schedule E will give you all the expenses they reported to the IRS. You will get this information during your due diligence period, after an offer is signed. Once you have a signed contract, the seller should allow you to inspect the property and the accounting records.

If you find something drastically different on the schedule E than was reported by the seller or calculated by you, you will need to do some investigating to understand the discrepancy.

Let's go over some of the areas of expenses you will need to consider that are not straightforward.

Accounting and legal: This area is different with every owner. Some do their own taxes and some prefer a CPA to do all the heavy lifting. I prefer to have a CPA. There are too many tax laws and too many yearly changes. I have enough work on my hands to keep up with the changing information in my own profession to worry about trying to keep up with the rental tax laws also.

I have had many one-on-one consultations with my CPA. When I venture into something new, I talk with him about the implications and the best way to move forward. Many times he has been the determining factor on handling tax and legal structure issues.

I have proposed several questions to both my CPA and my attorney that will impact accounting and legal expenses, such as these:

- Should I become an LLC or a corporation?

- Should I pay taxes as an S-corporation or a C-corporation?

- Do I need to have an employer identification number (EIN)?

- Do I need to send out 1099s?

You will want a good accountant and a good business attorney when you get into real estate. Get a feel for what they will be charging you for their services and factor that into your expenses, rather than using the seller's numbers.

Advertising: You will have vacancies each time a tenant moves out. When that happens, you will be advertising the vacancy to get a new tenant. How will you do that? If you use the local newspaper, it will cost some money. I used a sign in the yard and an ad in the local newspaper. My son used Craigslist. My method cost money, his method did not. Look at how the rental property in your area is being advertised and plan your expenses accordingly.

Business Expenses: There will be costs of running a business. You will need a phone, postage stamps, and paper to post notices. These expenses will tend to be small but not zero.

Eviction: Some tenants will stop paying rent and not move out. Others will become disruptive or not follow the rules. There will come a time when you need to evict a tenant. It doesn't happen very often, but it does happen. It costs me about $600 to evict a tenant. I don't do this myself. I hire it out. Even when I was managing the property myself, I hired out the evictions. I contacted a local property manager who was happy to take on an eviction, for a fee, and do all the right steps for me.

The courts have a very strict protocol and if a step or deadline is missed, the timeline will be reset and the tenant can stay even longer without paying rent. The property management company deals with the eviction courts frequently and will not miss a step or a deadline. As a busy professional, I do not have the time to show up in court for the eviction.

My grandmother always did her own evictions, but she had a lot of free time. I felt my time was better served in the office or the operating room than at the courthouse. Busy professionals should hire this out. Ask around and see what the fees will be and put a factor for this into your expenses.

Insurance: When you see what the seller was paying for insurance, you can expect your insurance bill to be a little higher. You will be getting a new policy and it is likely to be more than the seller's old policy. But it could also be lower if your timing is right.

Get at least three quotes from insurance companies. Policy premiums are based on the insurance company's losses for the previous year. If they had a big hit, their prices go up. When I get three quotes, I have found the difference between the lowest and highest could be more than double. You also may not be able to use your current insurance company. Not all insurance companies will cover rentals or commercial buildings.

Some insurance companies will make demands of you to do certain things with the property before they will insure it. If you don't like their demands, just go with another company who might not make such demands.

For one of my buildings, one company demanded the boiler room have a full inspection and certification before they would cover the building. I went with the company that didn't require me to take on that expense.

Management: This expense has the potential to be a game changer. Do you do the management yourself or pay someone else to do it? If you do it yourself, there will be some time involved in exchange for less expenses. If you hire a property manager or property management company, this could cost you as much as 10% of the rental income. That is a big swing in expenses.

It is not difficult or very time consuming to manage the property yourself. I will cover that in a later chapter. I managed 64 rental units as a full-time general surgeon. That saved me a lot of money in management fees. Later, when circumstances made it impractical for me to continue the management, I hired a manager and eventually a property management company to do the job.

The cost of management is not only the company's fee to manage the property—they also spend way more money on what they do than you might if you managed it yourself. For example, every spring, someone notices ants in their apartment and calls to have it taken care of. When I managed the place, I would swing by on the way home from the hospital and spray the perimeter of their apartment with pesticide and spray the area inside where the ants were entering. It took about 15 minutes of my time on the way home. If I didn't have time, my maintenance person would do it. The property management company will call a pest control company to come out. That is a minimum of $69. A 15-minute job that costs $69 works out to $276 an hour to do the job myself ($69 x 4 = $276).

When someone has a toilet with a flapper valve that needs replacing, my maintenance man would install a new one from the supply we keep in the office—or if he was not free, I could do it on the way home, a 10-minute job. The property management company charges me $60 to do it. They send someone out to check it, go to the store and get a flapper, and come back and put it in. A 10-minute job that pays $60 works out to $360 an hour to do the job myself ($60 x 6 = $360).

So when you figure the cost of management, add in some extra costs of maintenance to the figure they charge for a management fee. They tend to charge the fee as a percentage of rent collected, and they also charge for their time if anything is needed on the property.

Get a quote from more than one management company if you want to go that route. It is also nice if you can have the management company commit to a fixed rate to manage your property instead of a percentage of rents. That way when rents increase, your property management costs do not also increase.

The most conservative way to calculate management costs is to put in a management figure, even if you will be doing the management yourself. Something could happen and you need to switch to a management company. If you already figured in their commission cost, you will be fine.

Property taxes: Expect your property taxes to be higher than the seller has been paying. The value of a property tends to rise with time. County assessors tend to raise the taxes slower than the value of the property actually rises. Then when the property sells, they will reset the taxes. I think every property I bought had the property taxes increase the next year.

Don't forget property taxes are due once a year. Depending on when you buy a property, you may owe extra taxes at the time of purchase. In Oregon, property taxes are due in November and cover from June to June. If you buy a property in January, you will need to pay the property taxes from January to June during the purchase. If you buy in October, you will get a full property tax bill the month after you buy the place. Plan accordingly.

Repair and maintenance: You will need to come up with an estimate of what this figure will be. For my rentals, which are apartments about 40 years old and run by a property management company, the cost of repair and maintenance runs about $75 per unit per month. Back in 2002 when I was doing the maintenance myself, it cost about $30 per unit per month, but I had budgeted $50 per unit per month. The savings resulted from me doing a lot of the work myself.

You should ask around to other landlords in your area and find out what they are paying per unit per month for maintenance. If you do some of it yourself, you can lower the cost. If you have older units, you should increase the estimate. If you hire a property manager, you should increase the estimate. In a high cost-of-living area, these costs are also higher. After you own a few units, you will get a better feel for this cost.

NET OPERATING INCOME

Once you have calculated the estimated gross income and subtracted the total expenses, you will have the net operating income for the property. This is the amount of profit you would make if you paid cash for the property. Since it is less common to pay cash for this type of property, the NOI represents the total amount of money available to finance the property.

For every property you purchase, you must have a positive cash flow. To establish what your cash flow from the property would be, subtract the mortgage payments from the NOI.

There are so many different ways to finance a property that we will spend an entire chapter devoted to financing. Here are a few ideas to help you reach a positive cash flow.

WHAT TO DO IF THE INITIAL CALCULATION OF CASH FLOW IS NEGATIVE

If you make the initial calculations and the cash flow is negative, you have at least three choices to turn it to positive. How much above your expenses, including financing, that you want it will be up to you. The more the better, but everyone will have a different comfort zone.

LOWER THE PURCHASE PRICE

Knowing what NOI you have to work with, you can determine at what price you can afford to buy the property for it to be a positive cash flow.

For example, if the NOI of a property is $40,000 a year, that is $3,333.33 per month. Let's say you want to finance the property 100%, also known as a no-money-down deal. The financing you have lined up is a 6%, 30-year loan. A $556,000 loan under these terms is the maximum this property can support. You get this number by using an amortization calculator, found all over the internet. You put in the 6% and 30 years and then keep changing the loan total until you reach the monthly payment you need.

If you have decided the minimum cash flow for the property will be $300 a month or you will not make the deal, then you must buy the property for $50,000 under the maximum loan amount to create your desired cash flow because at 6% for 30 years, the cost of that borrowed $50,000 is $300 a month. So the maximum purchase price is $556,000 - $50,000 = $506,000. That will give you the $3,033 a month payment you need so you will have a $300 a month positive cash flow.

This means whatever the seller is asking, you cannot purchase the property as an investment unless you can get the price down to $506,000—which is the maximum amount you can borrow on this property and have $300 a month cash flow, with 100% financing.

MAKE A BIGGER DOWN PAYMENT

In the above example, you can only have a loan of $506,000 for the property to work (create the positive cash flow you want). The seller will only come down to $536,000. At this point you can change your mind about the no-money-down deal and put some money into the purchase.

If you were to put $30,000 into the deal as a down payment, that gives the seller the purchase price she wants and gives you the loan amount you need based on the NOI. The deal would now have a 5.6% down payment for a $300-per-month positive cash flow.

GET BETTER TERMS ON THE LOAN

In the above example, if the seller won't come down below $536,000, you can still swing the deal at no money down if you can negotiate a lower interest rate on the loan. If you can get the loan at 5.47% for 30 years, you will bring the payments on the $536,000 loan down to the $3,033 you need to make the deal work for you. You will need an amortization calculator to figure this out.

As you can see, once you know the NOI, you know what you need to do to make the property an investment. You have some variables to work with to make a viable deal.

Never buy property under terms that make your cash flow negative.

Here is where the other calculations you made in valuing the property come into play. If you want to offer less than the seller is asking, you may be able to make the offer and show the seller why you feel the property is worth less than the asking price. The comps might not support the price or the cap rate could be too low. Either way, if you can support why the price needs to be lower for the deal to work, it will help the seller move down in price.

Never forget there is no right or wrong answer for the absolute value of a property. You always have some leeway. You have determined the terms you need and even then, you could offer different amounts and still make the deal work for you, depending on how you manipulate the variables of price, down payment, and terms of the financing. Don't get stuck on only one way to buy the property. There is always more than one way to proceed with a win-win deal.

Beware of analysis paralysis. Don't spend so much time going over the numbers and playing with different ways to make the offer that you never actually make the offer. While you are busy figuring out what you want to do, someone else may be buying the property.

WALK AWAY IF IT DOESN'T WORK

Make your calculations, then either make an offer or walk away, but don't dally. You are a busy professional. You do not have time to play around with this too much. Make your best calculations and act. Walking away is often hard once you invest time into the project. You must learn to let go of the ones that don't work so you will be able to find the ones that do work.

I once talked with a seller about buying their property and part of the deal would require some owner financing. I wanted a balloon payment at least 10 years into the future. The seller was not willing to go more than 5 years. I felt 5 years was not safe enough for a balloon term. So I walked away from the deal.

The realtor pestered me to put the offer in writing to try and force a deal. I did not have the time to waste making offers that would not fly. I only make offers that I feel represent a win-win deal and have a good chance of being accepted. I had a hard time convincing the realtor that if the seller met with me in good faith to discuss terms, then making an offer that did not follow our discussion was not appropriate. If I was going to do that, I could have just made the offer in the first place to see what would happen.

Chapter 8

HOW TO FINANCE REAL ESTATE INVESTMENT PROPERTY

Financing your real estate purchase is one of the most misunderstood topics in real estate investing. I see it time and again. The object of buying the investment real estate is to create wealth. If you already have money to buy apartments with cash, you already have wealth. We all start somewhere and need to borrow the money to begin a real estate portfolio.

Many people talk about starting with single-family homes because they don't have enough money to put 30% down on an apartment. When I hear that, I realize they don't understand financing real estate. They have only heard of one way to buy a property and that is to pay 30% cash as a down payment and the bank will loan you the rest.

That is only one of hundreds of ways to finance a property. And it is one of the most cumbersome and most expensive of all the choices. I suspect if you walked down the street and asked

100 people what it takes to buy a rental property, 95% of them would give this conventional answer. And that is why they call it conventional financing.

I have never used conventional financing to buy an investment property, and each deal has been different. When I bring that up in conversation, I get puzzled looks. Then the same questions come, again and again.

"How can you buy a rental without 30% down?"

"So you used owner financing, then?"

Then when I tell them most of the deals were no money down and I got cash back at closing, I hear something like these statements:

"You can't do that since the banking changes after the 2008 real estate crash."

"I've heard about shady deals like that."

"No money down is too risky."

Since most people have never been exposed to an alternative way to buy real estate, they are surprised when they find out someone has done it.

Let's go over the conventional way of financing investment real estate so we have a reference point.

CONVENTIONAL FINANCING

The term "all cash" needs to be qualified. It means different things to different people. If I am the seller, all cash means I got all my money in cash and it doesn't matter where the cash came from. If I am the buyer, all cash means either I paid all my own money or the seller did not carry the loan. If I am the bank, it means no money was borrowed to make the deal. Sometimes when you see "requires all cash" in an advertisement, it means the property will not qualify for bank financing.

But a no-money-down deal from the buyer's point of view can look to the seller like all cash, since he got a check for the entire amount. Conventional financing, from the seller's point of view, is an all-cash deal that gets delayed for the financing to be completed. So don't get confused by that term. It means different things at different times.

For most people, the only place they know to get the big dollars they need for a real estate purchase is from the bank. And the bank knows they have you as a captive audience. You do not have another option as far as they know, so they get to dictate the terms. They have control.

The bank will tell you how much your minimum down payment will be. They will decide what the interest rate will be. And for the privilege of loaning you this money, they will tack on a lot of fees like points, loan origination fees, and appraisals. He who has the gold makes the rules.

Not only are the terms for conventional loans dictated by the bank, they are often dictated by someone from another state. If you go to The U.S. First National Interstate Bank and ask for a loan, the loan officer will have a set of rules they must follow. They cannot stray from the rules.

If you go to The People's Evergreen Valley Bank of Bedford Falls, the CEO of the bank is in the building. He has the ability to look at your individual case and make some exceptions to the rules.

As an example, one investor I know purchased his first investment property one year earlier with no money down. The property had been making a profit every month for the past year. When he went to the national bank for a home loan to buy his first personal residence, they turned him down. He did not qualify for the loan because of the bank's rules for handling his real estate investment.

During the first two years of a real estate investment, according to many banks, only the mortgage payments count. They will not count any of the income coming from the property until it has a two-year track record. So even though the property generated positive cash flow every month, it counted against him as a negative cash flow expense. They considered his real estate investment a second mortgage (after the home loan), and his income couldn't support both loans.

That rule is, of course, ridiculous. To disregard the income coming in from the property is not appropriate. So he went to a local bank. The local bank had the same general rule. But they were able to look at him specifically. Looking at the rental history, his personal finance history, and the future purchase, he certainly qualified for the loan. They gave him the mortgage for his personal residence.

The bank will also make you jump through a lot of hoops. You will fill out a lot of paperwork. You will need to provide your last two tax returns and proof of your accounts with other banks for the last two months. In some cases, they will make you bring in a tax return and fill out net worth information on an annual basis as long as you have the loan.

The entire process will take 6-12 weeks to complete. Once, I was trying to refinance a property and the bank was dragging their feet. I finally went in and demanded to know why this wasn't finished yet. That's when I found out the truth. They were waiting to find out what would happen to another loan—that I had no knowledge of—from a company I was associated with, who was working on a loan problem. Because both of these issues were happening in the same bank, they had my name associated with the other entity. They would not make the refinance loan on my property until the unrelated issue with the other company was complete. If I had picked any other bank to do the refinance with, they would have never known about this other issue. I was furious that they didn't tell me this in the first place. They didn't because they knew I would just go to a different bank and they would lose the loan.

Dealing with a bank can be very cumbersome. They want to make safe loans for them, and that is why they require 30% down. The percentage varies a little from bank to bank but will be in that neighborhood.

If you had zero down payment and the bank financed 100% of the property, they know you have no skin in the game. If something goes wrong, you could just walk away and leave them holding the bag. Many people have done that. The value of a property drops below the loan value and the owner just leaves and give it back to the bank. This is very unethical. It may be legal, but it is not ethical. You agreed to pay, so you should pay if you can.

The point is, a no-money-down deal is a risk to the bank, not a risk to you. You have no money at risk. The more you invest as a down payment, the higher your risk of money lost if something goes wrong. However, the more money you put down, the lower the chances something will go wrong.

For conventional financing, you will have to have good credit to get good terms. If your credit is not good, they may not loan you anything at all. If conventional financing is all you know and all you try, you will be very limited in what you can buy.

Many banks will not want to lend money to your LLC. They don't want your limited liability to mean you won't have to pay back the loan if a problem happens. You will often need to make a personal guarantee on the loan for the bank to be happy dealing with an LLC.

There are a lot of deals out on the market that say something like "property will not qualify for financing." That only means there is something about the property that will not fall into the bank's rulebook, so they cannot touch it. The reason for these rules is the bank wants to be sure they can sell the house quickly if they repossess it. So anything that can slow down a sale can be a cause for the bank to be unwilling to finance it. Since you are buying a property for the long haul, many of these reasons the bank won't provide financing do not matter to you.

Some examples:

Too many repairs are needed. If a property is a fixer, the bank may not want it for fear of getting it back only half fixed. If you plan on fixing everything and then renting it for years, it won't matter to you.

Roof needs replacing. Often a bank will not loan on a property that needs a new roof. Once you put on the new roof the issue is gone.

No bathroom. If the prior tenants took the toilet and sink out of the building and now it doesn't have a functioning bathroom, a bank might not loan on the property. You will be fixing it so it's OK for you.

These are things that might make a bank unwilling to loan on the property but are not necessarily a bad thing for you. You could use that as leverage to get a better deal from the seller. Then fix the stuff, rent the place, and you are on your way.

Even though there is so much hassle with conventional financing, you should still have it as an option. You need to establish a good relationship with a bank and their loan officer so you are a known investor and they want your business. You may use conventional financing, and you will likely refinance somewhere along your journey, so treat the bank nicely.

Do not use any of the calculations the bank shows you to make decisions on your purchase as an investment. The bank is not looking at the property as an investment for you. They are looking at the property as an investment for them. Cash flow is the important thing to you. Resale if you default on the loan is the important thing for the bank.

UNCONVENTIONAL FINANCING

Any way you finance a property that is not a down payment with a bank mortgage will fall into the unconventional category. My first purchase was a good example. I financed it 100% using a combination of owner carry, signature loan from the bank that was not tied to the property, personal loan from a relative, and a loan from the realtor. I literally got paid to take over the property, which is the essence of no money down with cash back at closing.

There are many ways to come up with the money to make a real estate purchase and I will show you a few examples here. You have already calculated your NOI so you know how much money you have to work with to make the deal yield a positive cash flow.

Once you have the NOI figure, any loan payment arrangement that will finance the property without going over that number will work. I love the example of this concept from the movie *Apollo 13*.

After the explosion on their spacecraft, the Apollo 13 astronauts had to get home. Any combination of actions they took that got them home would be good. At one point they realized they were low on battery power. To conserve energy, they shut down everything that was not absolutely essential. Then it came time to power up the craft for reentry.

There was a limited amount of battery power to do the job. Back on the ground, one astronaut was in the simulator trying to figure out how to start up the ship with the limits the batteries placed on them. They could not use the conventional procedure and needed to come up with a new way to do it.

After trying many different ways, they found one that would work. It restarted the systems in an order the batteries could handle and got the astronauts home.

Think of the NOI as the limited amount of power you have to pay for the financing of a property. Any deal that works within the NOI and puts the property in your portfolio will work. Then you will have years of cash flow and appreciation working for you. You will also be able to take advantage of the depreciation.

So let's say you are buying a small apartment complex with an NOI of $52,000. You determine you want a positive cash flow of $4,000 to make the deal. That means you need financing that will cost no more than $48,000 per year ($4,000 per month) and the seller has agreed to consider seller financing. The following loan options will all work and will feel equivalent to you, but not to the seller.

THIRTY-YEAR LOAN AMOUNT WITH $4,000/MONTH PAYMENT BASED ON INTEREST RATE

Interest Rate (%)	Loan Amount ($)
8.0	545,134
7.5	572,070
7.0	601,230
6.5	632,844
6.0	667,166
5.5	704,487
5.0	745,126
4.5	789,445
4.0	837,845
3.5	890,780
3.0	948,757
2.5	1,012,348
2.0	1,082,195
1.5	1,159,015
1.0	1,243,627
0.5	1,336,945
0.0	1,440,000

As you can see, as the interest rate goes up, the amount of the mortgage goes down in order to keep the payment constant. Any mortgage loan calculator will give you these figures. I have used this method to give the seller flexibility as to how they collect the profit. If they take a higher price and lower interest, they collect more money as capital gains and less as interest. If they take a lower total sale price but higher interest rate, they collect more interest and less capital gains.

The sweet spot is in the middle of this list. As you move up the list, interest rate climbs and the loan amount falls. So if you were to pay off the loan early, the seller gets less money. As you move down the list, interest rate falls and the loan size increases. The buyer will have no incentive to pay the loan off early and will be in debt the entire 30 years. Use the center and move up and down a little to make the deal work. In general it is best to stay away from the extreme ends of this chart. Changing the interest rate by 0.5% could mean the difference between positive and negative cash flow.

If the owner was selling for $720,000, for example, the $4,000 payment would be at 5.3% interest. You could also offer either $704,487 for a 5.5% loan or you could give them $745,126, which is more than the asking price, if they would do the loan at 5.0%. Many sellers would jump at the chance to sell for more than the asking price for a slightly lower interest rate on the loan. Moving toward more capital gains and less interest income is better for the seller because capital gains are taxed at a lower rate. (This leaves any down payment out of the calculations for simplicity.)

Depending on their situation, one of the two options might weigh more on their mind. Some sellers are locked in on a price. You can show them the options and tell them you can pay the asking price if they give you seller financing at a lower interest rate. They may like selling at the asking price better than getting a higher interest rate.

Other owners are really interested in getting good interest rates, so they like to see the high interest numbers and will take a lower price to get the interest rate they want. They might ask for a prepayment penalty to assure you will pay them the interest they want for the period they want.

To you, all these deals are essentially the same. It will cost you $4,000 a month. This option may make or break a deal. If the loan options are all for 30 years and you never make an extra payment, you will pay the exact same amount of money for each option: $1,440,000. Which is $4,000 a month x 12 months a year x 30 years.

You can see from this example that good terms on a loan can make up for a higher price. In the long run, you just need to stay within the $4,000 parameter and you own the property.

SELLER FINANCING

Seller financing is my favorite way to buy a property. In fact, I like it so well, I once rejected a potential property because it still had a significant mortgage on it. I wanted the possibility of seller financing to be on the table. I have been able to show sellers who did not want to do seller financing that they would be a lot better off taking this route than taking all cash.

If they take all cash, they will have to do something with the money anyway. If they are interested in investing the money in interest-bearing vehicles like bonds, CDs, or money market accounts, then why not collect the interest from me and get a better rate than the bank is offering? Many times they like the idea once they think it through. Here is where knowing about the seller's plans can come in handy.

Seller financing is less expensive up front. Banks charge many fees that add to the deal that you won't have with seller financing. These include but are not limited to points, loan origination fees, mortgage insurance, and appraisals.

Seller financing is simpler. I have never had a seller do a credit check on me, ask me for my last two year's tax returns, or ask for proof of funds and a net worth calculation. If a seller did ask for those things, it would be reasonable to provide them since they are extending credit to me. Sellers usually don't care about my creditworthiness. They know the property, and if you as the buyer default, they take it back to sell again and keep any money you have already paid.

Seller financing is more flexible. As you saw in the chart above, you and the owner can work out any kind of terms you both agree upon. Banks will want a balloon at 10 years, if it is a commercial loan, and I only had two sellers ever consider a balloon on the loan.

Sellers will make interest-only deals, which lowers your monthly payment and increases your cash flow. I had one seller who made a deal for a minimum payment of interest only for 30 years, with a balloon of the remaining balance at the end of the 30 years. For me that was great. It gave me the lowest possible payment for the entire loan term. I paid interest only for several years and when the rents had gone up enough, making my cash flow larger, I started making bigger payments. In fact, I began making payments at an amount that would have the loan paid off by the 30-year mark so the balloon payment would be zero. Thus my payments increased as my NOI increased.

When I recently sold a piece of property, I offered a similar loan to the new buyer. I offered five years of interest only and then the loan would amortize for 30 years. That gave her a lower payment for five years. Any extra payments she made during that time would result in a lower payment for her during those final 30 years. She loved the loan terms and looked no further for a place to buy. Her realtor said, "Wow, those are great terms." I will get a fixed interest for 35 years if she doesn't pay it off early. I would be 91 years old by then. It's like having an annuity without dealing with an insurance agent.

Seller financing is quicker, so you can often close escrow in as little as a week. Sellers will be more flexible on the down payment. Banks have a boiler plate they must follow for loans.

As you can see, there are great advantages to seller financing, yet most people never consider it. As a buyer, I can't think of a single disadvantage. Maybe the owner will not sign off on the loan at the end of the term. That can be avoided by going through a loan servicing company. They will take care of the loan and certify that it is paid off in the end. In some cases I have paid the seller the payments directly, and in other cases we used an intermediary loan-servicing company. I make the payments to the loan-servicing company and they keep track of the outstanding balance and send the payment forward to the seller. They do charge a few dollars each month for the service. Do whichever makes you and the seller more comfortable.

MONEY FROM OTHER PROPERTY

Another unconventional source of funding is using the equity from other properties you own. There are several ways to do this.

First, you could get a new mortgage on a property you currently own. If you have significant equity in the property, a new mortgage could pay off the old mortgage and leave you with some cash for the next deal. As an example, if your property currently has an appraised valued at $250,000 and the mortgage is down to $80,000, the new mortgage could be taken out for 70% of the appraised value, which is $175,000. After paying off the old mortgage, you would have $95,000 in cash to use for the next deal. Always be sure your cash flow will still be positive after the refinance.

You could also use the other property as collateral for a 100% owner-financed deal. Say you want to buy Property A for $200,000 and the seller doesn't need the cash but is leery of 100% financing. You also own Property B free and clear, which is worth $150,000. You could give the owner a wraparound mortgage, putting both properties up for collateral on the loan. Then the seller sells you the property with 100% financing but has $350,000 of collateral for his $200,000 loan. This makes him feel more secure and you own both properties without needing a down payment.

If the owner doesn't want the deal, the bank will take it. You can finance Property A for 70%, which comes to $140,000. You could get the other $60,000 needed for the deal by taking a loan out on Property B, which is only 40% loan to value.

Whatever you do, don't borrow money against your personal residence to make real estate investments. You do not want to put your home at risk for an investment. If something were to go wrong, it's no big deal to lose your investment. It's a big deal to lose your home.

I remember the following conversation:

"Is it OK to take a second mortgage out on your home to make a really, really great investment?"

"What does your wife think?"

"I withdraw the question."

Making investments is not worth putting your home at risk.

MONEY FROM OTHER PEOPLE

Friends, relatives, and other investors make a great source of investment funds. Other physicians who control their retirement accounts can use the money to make property loans. Many retired people want better interest to live on, so they can be a source of capital.

Several years ago, one of my grandmother's rentals had a fireplace fall and the property was condemned. Her insurance company paid to rebuild the house.

She then had a brand-new house and decided to sell it instead of rent it. She came to me and wanted to know what ideas I had for where she could put the money and collect interest. I looked around and the best I could find at the time was about 1%. I wanted to come up with something better for her.

I realized I had some mortgages on investment property at 5% interest. The bank was essentially paying Grandma 1% on her money and then loaning it to me for 5%. I began to wonder how I could cut out the middleman—the bank—on the deal.

The smallest mortgage I had was about double what she wanted to invest. I proposed to her that if I could come up with the funding for the rest of the mortgage, we could cut out the bank and she and the other investors could take over the mortgage and get the 5% I was currently paying the bank.

I contacted a few other friends and relatives with the idea. They were all sick of getting 0.01% interest on their cash. They lived on that money and wanted a better deal. Many of them liked the idea. I raised more cash than I needed, paid off the bank, and began paying the interest to my friends and relatives instead. I was able to transfer $22,500 per year in interest to my friends and relatives with just the stroke of a pen. That mortgage was money I was already paying anyway. Why pay it to the bank when I could pay it to my grandmother and relatives instead?

Since I raised more than I needed, I kept the process going and retired all the loans I had from a bank. Today, my friends and relatives are collecting the interest I used to pay the banks. Everyone is happy. Except maybe the bank.

LIFE INSURANCE

If you made a mistake and purchased a whole life insurance policy in the past and now you are not willing to give up the policy, you can put the cash value to good use.

The salesman who talked you into this poor deal can now be useful. You can take a loan out from the cash value of the policy and use that money for capital in a real estate deal. That would make a lousy insurance policy useful for something.

THE PROPERTY ITSELF

Don't forget about the value of the property itself. For example, let's say you wanted to buy a rental house on five acres. The backside of the property has old timber on it. You could make a contract with a logging company to come in and log the property. The payment from the timber company could be used for the down payment on the house and the rest could be financed through any other method.

PARTNERS

Another great source of cash for a deal is partners. You might consider buying a property that will require you to put in $200,000 cash, but you only have $100,000. You can join with a partner who also has $100,000 in cash and buy the property together.

I have made several deals with partners. Partners make it easier to do bigger deals you might not have been able to finance yourself. However, there are some distinct disadvantages to having partners. Partners do not always agree on things.

LOOK FOR COMMON GOALS

Partners often do not all have the same goal in mind. For this reason it is best to find partners who have a similar financial situation. If you mix partners who are 65 years old with partners who are 35 years old, you might create some conflict.

A few years from now when the place needs a new roof, the older partners will be retired and want good cash flow so they won't want to put money into the roof. In fact, they might want to sell the place. The younger partners will still be working and won't mind the roof expense.

I faced this recently when someone came along and offered to buy a building I was a partner in. Some partners wanted the good cash flow coming off the building. Others wanted to get the cash infusion that we would create by selling. This caused a rift among the owners. We voted on the deal and the majority won, but there were still some hard feelings from those who wanted the vote to go the other way.

KEEP YOUR EYES OPEN

There are many sources of money out there. Some are good sources and some are not. You do not want to get into borrowing from companies that prey on people with poor credit. These companies have ads that say things like, "Will loan money for property," "Bad credit, no problem," and "We have money to lend."

The reason you want to avoid them is the high interest they charge. They want to finance deals for people with bad credit who can't get a good loan. They also want to repossess the property if they can. They either make great interest off you or get the property. Either way, it is not a good deal for you.

Financing your property is not a mystery, but it must fit within the NOI. Go conventional or unconventional. Either way, you end up with the property and all the future income and appreciation belongs to your portfolio.

Don't ignore any source of cash, such as selling a boat you no longer need or that treadmill you are using as a clothes rack.

NO-MONEY-DOWN DEALS

What about buying the property with no money down? Can it be done today?

The first time I heard of this idea was when I began to shop for my first property. I bought it with no money down and cash back at closing. Yet I have heard and read from many sources that this doesn't work, can't be done, or is too risky.

Even today, 18 years later and after the real estate crash of 2008 when they changed banking rules, I still hear the same thing. You can't buy a property with no money down. Well, it isn't true.

I know of deals that have been done recently for no money down. So it is as viable today as it was in the past. And people are still out there who tell you it won't work.

The key to no-money-down purchases is to be clear on the NOI. Once you know the NOI for the property, if you can stay within that parameter and still buy the property fully financed, then it is a good deal.

I showed a few examples in a previous section on unconventional financing. Let's go over the basics so it is clear.

Let's use an apartment purchase for $500,000 as an example. If the owner is willing to carry $400,000 with good terms, then you subtract those payments from the NOI you calculated. What remains of the NOI is what you have to work with in financing the other $100,000 that the owner wants in cash.

The source of the money is not relevant, only that it fits within the NOI. The realtor could loan you her commission of $15,000, a fellow physician could loan you $50,000 from their retirement plan, and the remaining $35,000 could come from a second mortgage on another property.

As long as all of the payments on the loans stay within your NOI, you are golden.

When real estate prices are relatively high, fewer properties will work with a no-money-down deal. When prices are low, more of them are available. You don't need to find a lot of them—you only need to find one.

If you can't swing no money down and you still want the property, then simply put enough down payment into the deal to bring the mortgage payments into the size that fits with the NOI.

WHAT ABOUT RISK WITH NO MONEY DOWN?

There is some inherent risk to buying property, except in two situations: 100% financed or 0% financed.

The only no-risk deals are those that you don't have any money invested to lose or you don't have any loan to be foreclosed on. Everything in between has some risk of foreclosure.

Your risk can be minimized by carefully assessing the property, calculating the net operating income, carrying fire insurance, and financing with safe terms. Those terms include never getting an adjustable rate mortgage, avoiding balloon payments less than 10 years in the future, and buying for the long haul.

Work to minimize the risks, keep your property for a long time, and you will find investing in real estate to be very rewarding.

REFINANCE BEFORE RETIREMENT

One thing to keep in mind about financing a property is you can do it again and again, if the situation warrants it.

If interest rates drop a few years after you buy the property, you can refinance the loan, but be aware of prepayment penalties. Every time you refinance, you can increase the cash flow of the property. But don't forget to include the costs of refinancing, as no one will do this for free.

Avoid taking equity out of the property unless you have a really good reason to do so, such as to use as the down payment on another property. Getting the money to buy a new motorhome, boat, or motorcycle is never a good reason to refinance a property. You are trying to maximize your cash flow for a future retirement, so you want to avoid harvesting any equity.

The final year before you retire from your profession, while your income is still high and you look great on paper, is a good time to refinance and bump up your cash flow to use in retirement.

RETIREMENT REFINANCE EXAMPLE

Let's say you have a property with an initial $500,000 loan for 30 years at 6% interest. The monthly payments on the loan are $2,997.75. You have owned the property for 15 years and made some extra payments with your bonus checks along the way, so now the loan balance is down to $200,000. You are planning to retire in six months.

This is a great time to refinance the loan to increase your retirement income. If interest rates are the same, the new $200,000 30-year mortgage would cost $1,199.10 per month. The difference between the old loan payment and the new one is $1,798.65, or $21,583.80 a year. That is a nice retirement income boost for filling out a few papers.

This move will reset the loan to another 30 years but will increase your cash flow in return and give you a better income during retirement. This is the kind of loan it's OK to carry into your retirement, as it is funding your retirement. Yes, you will pay more interest in the long run by extending the mortgage and starting your 30 years again, but when you retire, the long-term interest cost is not as important as having enough cash flow to live on. If you don't need more cash flow, then you don't need to refinance.

"Progress always involves risk.
You can't steal second base and
keep your foot on first."

— Fred Wilcox

Chapter 9

MAKING THE OFFER

Once you have done the cash flow method to evaluate the investment potential of the property and considered the financing, you are ready to make an offer.

Many real estate books and people who talk about real estate are trying to get you to make a lot of offers. You might hear things like, "It takes 20-30 offers before you get a yes," or "You've got to throw a lot of mud on the wall and see what sticks." I totally disagree with this approach to real estate investing. This is actually just bargain hunting and is similar to going to many garage sales looking for something where the seller doesn't realize the true value. Speculators want to use this method, as they are after short-term profits.

As a busy professional, you can't afford the time it takes to make lots of offers and go bargain hunting. This very factor may be what keeps many professionals from getting into real estate investing. What you need to do is look for valuable long-term investments, not bargains. Bargains are for flippers. Bargains are simply a bonus to a busy professional, not a dealmaker.

Never forget the example I gave earlier about the purchase of a house in 1975. The value of that property 40 years later makes the purchase price less significant. At the time of purchase, it may seem like a great bargain to buy the house for 30% less, and it is. But 40 years later, it won't make much difference which price you paid as long as the cash flow was positive. Forty years of cash flow and 40 years of appreciation will be a lot of money in your purse.

MAKE GOOD OFFERS

Only make offers on property you think would be good for you to own for 40-plus years. Don't mistake this statement to mean if you are 70 years old then you shouldn't buy real estate. Positive and growing cash flow is money in your pocket at any age. The appreciation you will get over 40 years is a nice bonus, but it is not what you are after.

Only make win-win offers. Don't try to lowball sellers. You don't have the time to waste on declined offers—and neither do the sellers.

Following this principle, I was able to purchase about 50% of the properties on which I made offers. That is a much better use of my time than making 20 offers to get one deal. Use a good screening process and teach your realtor well, and you will not waste a lot of time making offers that get turned down.

The other issue you must contend with in making offers is your reputation. As a busy professional in your community, you want a good reputation. You don't want to be known as a cheapskate, a slumlord, or a wheeler-dealer. Make offers you can back up with figures and be proud of.

I have seen many pieces of real estate that were priced so high it was not worth making an offer. I often talked with the seller and told them why I couldn't make a deal at that price. Then I said if they ever wanted to consider something near what I was figuring, they could give me a call. I never got any of those calls.

I was once in on a business deal put together by one person, which involved a lot of partners. There was one guy in town I thought really needed to be in on the deal. I asked him why he was not interested. His answer gave me pause. He said, "I've seen the kind of deals he makes and I'll have no part of them."

The person in question had made some deals in the past that were giving him a bad reputation. You cannot afford to tarnish your professional reputation with real estate deals that might leave a bad taste in someone's mouth. Word gets out and bad press gets around a lot faster than good press. So keep your nose clean.

GET TO KNOW THE SELLER

I believe the most important part of making an offer is knowing the seller and the seller's needs. I always try to meet the seller in person. If the seller knows the property, I like to walk the property with the seller and have a nice conversation with them about the property and what they will be doing with the proceeds of the sale. I only do this if the property has already been evaluated and looks like a positive cash flow, so I'm considering the purchase. I don't want to waste my time or the seller's time with this walk-through unless I think I can make the deal happen.

Of the five apartment complexes I bought, I was able to do this with four of them. The other was inherited by the kids of the owner and they did not want to talk and just wanted the proceeds in their pocket. Of the properties I considered and did not end up owning, I was able to get to know the seller about half of the time. Not all sellers want to talk with you. They may want their realtor to handle everything. It doesn't mean you can't make a deal; it is just one less arrow in your quiver.

In the earlier story of my first purchase, I was able to learn that the seller needed enough money to buy a sailboat, pay off his house, and sail around the world. That was very important information for me to use in making an offer.

When talking about the property, don't bad-mouth the seller or the property. No seller wants you to tell them why the property sucks. They already know the bad points of the property. Many people like pointing these out to make a case for driving down the price. What you really do is tick off the seller with your attitude and make them not very interested in negotiating with you.

If you like the seller and the seller likes you, you will have a much nicer negotiating process and are likely to come up with a win-win deal. If you tick off the seller, they will not be interested in giving you any concessions.

DON'T SEND PAPER OFFERS BACK AND FORTH

Realtors are notorious for putting an offer in writing and then batting those offers and counter offers back and forth, creating a massive pile of papers. Try to avoid that.

Make your first offer either verbally or as a letter of intent. Then, when you have the basic parts agreed upon by both parties, put the offer into writing and present it to the seller in person. I have said, "Rather than sending a bunch of paperwork back and forth, let's talk this through and see what we can come up with and then put that into writing." Most realtors do not like this, but most sellers do. Face to face is always the best way to avoid miscommunications. Since you are not trying to take advantage of the seller or gouge or lowball them, this should be a positive impression.

When putting together a letter of intent, you might give the seller some options to choose from. Having three choices to pick from makes the seller more likely to pick one of them. Having one option means the seller must take or reject it and possibly make a counteroffer. Here is a sample letter of intent. It is short, simple, and to the point and will save a lot of negotiating time.

Bob,

Thanks for showing me your property yesterday. I enjoyed our conversation. I am interested in moving forward with buying your property. I am able to proceed with one of the following scenarios. Choose the option that's best for you and I will have my realtor write up the official offer with a $1,000 earnest money deposit.

A: All cash and close in seven days with a purchase price of $350,000.

B: I can finance the property and offer you $400,000 and we can close in three months.

C: I can offer $435,000 with a $35,000 cash down payment and seller financing of the balance at 5% for 30 years ($2,147 per month), and we can close in seven days.

Let me know which of these offers is best for you and we can proceed. If you need to discuss anything about this, give me a call at (503) 123-4567. Looking forward to hearing your response in the next 48 hours.

Cory Fawcett

A letter of intent is not a binding contract. It is a way of making some of the big decisions early so both parties understand what they want. If none of these offers are even close to what the seller wants, you can save yourself the trouble of the 30-page real estate offer and all the counteroffers. If a letter of intent is good, then you can write up an offer that will have minimal counteroffers and save yourself a lot of time.

I always put my contact information on things so the seller can contact me directly, if they want, without going through their realtor. This will save a lot of time and hassle. Sellers like this option. Realtors do not want buyers and sellers speaking without the realtor being in the conversation. Always remember the person in charge is not the realtor.

WRITING THE OFFER

When it comes time to write an offer, if you are using a realtor, she will have a set form her office uses. It will be ridiculously long and cover all kinds of things. You must read the entire contract. Every word.

Do not bow to the temptation of saying it is a standard offer and skip reading it. There is nothing standard about an offer form. It is the form your particular real estate office uses and you can change almost anything on the form to suit your needs. Just because it is preprinted doesn't mean you can't cross out parts that don't work. Don't fall for any of the "it has to be in the contract" stuff your realtor might say.

You could write your own contract stating something like this:

"I, Cory Fawcett, agree to buy John Smith's property located at 123 Elm St. in Paducah, Kentucky, for the sum of $100,000, all cash, to close seven days from acceptance."

That would be a perfectly good real estate purchase contract if both parties agree. So there is nothing in the multipage form the realtor uses that can't be crossed off. But all of the words on their contract are there for a reason. Most of the time, that reason is to protect the seller, as most real estate contracts are designed with the seller's best interests in mind. After all, the realtors are working for the seller who is paying their fee.

Let's go over some of the things you want to consider in your offer.

EARNEST MONEY

Almost all offers should include some earnest money. This is to signify that you are serious about the purchase. If you back out for no good reason, you will lose the earnest money. This is fair since your offer ties up the property and the owner can't sell it to someone else while in escrow with you. If you back out, they might have missed another buyer in the process so the earnest money compensates them for their loss.

I always use $1,000 for my earnest money. I give it initially as a promissory note stating I agree to deposit the money into escrow within 48 hours of acceptance of the offer. That way I don't tie up any real money until there is a deal agreed on.

Your realtor may tell you it is customary to put 10% as an earnest money offer. I simply say my custom is $1,000. The seller might come back with a counteroffer for more earnest money, but more than likely they will let your figure ride. If they counter, you can discuss how much earnest money will make the seller comfortable and decide if you are willing to increase your earnest money.

OFFER PRICE

If you had a letter of intent with three offer options, you can put in the option they chose. If you didn't use a letter of intent, you can include those three options in the offer contract. Simply state "See Addendum A" in the slot for a price and Addendum A will have the three choices for the seller.

FIXTURES AND PERSONAL PROPERTY

In the offer, list everything that is not attached to the property and anything that is attached that they might take. Some things you might list that you want included in the deal: washing machines, dryers, stoves, dishwashers, refrigerators, lawn mower, awnings, furniture, barbecue, irrigation pump, garage door openers, patio furniture, ski boat, yard gnome, or any-thing else you want included.

If they don't want to include it, they will say so in the counter-offer. If you throw in a few things that don't matter to you, you will either get something extra, or you will have something easy to let go of during negotiations.

FINANCING CONTINGENCIES

It is very important that your offer includes contingencies. These are things that can allow you to get out of the offer and get your earnest money back if you don't like something. There are many things that still need to happen after the offer is ac-cepted, and if they don't go well you want a way out. One of those is financing.

You do not want to be locked into an offer if you can't get the financing to complete the offer. Your financing contingencies should state the terms you need. For example, "This offer is contingent on the buyer and the property qualifying for 80% financing at an interest rate of 5% or less and the appraisal coming in at the purchase price or higher."

This gives you an out if the financing comes in at 5.5% and you don't want to pay that much. Then you can walk away from the deal and get your earnest money back.

If owner financing is on the table, you should spell out all the terms. Use an addendum if needed. An example might be owner to carry a note for $400,000, interest only, at 5% for the first five years and the monthly payments would be $1,666.67. After five years, the remaining principal shall be amortized over 30 years with interest rate of 5% with no prepayment penalties, payments due on the 10th of each month with a $50 late fee if payment is more than five days late.

The title company handling the escrow will write up the formal loan agreements based on what you stated in the offer.

Be aware that since the 2008 crash, there are new laws in place affecting seller financing. Please check your state laws to see how it might affect you. This is where having a good attorney on your team comes in handy.

1031 EXCHANGE TIMING

If some of the proceeds for this purchase are coming from a 1031 exchange, be sure to state it and allow for extra time to close. Set the closing date for at least 10 days after the closing date of the 1031 exchange's other transaction. There are times when these transactions get delayed and you need time to react.

REQUEST SCHEDULE E

Every time you purchase a rental property, ask for proof of how the property has been doing. This is either the owner's schedule

E on the last two years' tax returns or if the property has its own tax return, you need to see the last two of those.

The reason you need to see two years is the owner could have tried to keep costs down during the last year by delaying non-urgent repairs to show you a different story than reality. It would be hard for them to do that two years in a row.

If they are unwilling to show this to you, you should be very cautious about buying that property. There is no reason to keep this information from you. You are not asking them for their entire personal tax returns, only for the one page (schedule E) that has all the rental property income and expenses.

INSURANCE CONTINGENCY

The buyer (you) must provide proof of fire insurance by the close of escrow. Get started on the insurance as soon as the deal is signed. Get at least three quotes for insurance. If you can't get an insurance company to insure the property, you want to be able to walk away and get your earnest money back.

INSPECTION RESULTS CONTINGENCY

This is a key contingency. You want to be able to inspect the place and back out of the deal if something turns up you don't like. There are two ways to inspect: either do it yourself or hire someone to do it for you. You will need to specify a time frame to get the inspection done and how long you will have to accept the results of the inspection.

You should have something about backing out such as, if the inspection finds more than $500 worth of needed repairs, you can renegotiate. This can be worded as "Buyer will accept up to $500 worth of repairs needed per the inspection results."

Be sure you or your inspector sees every unit of a multi-unit complex. Sometimes the one they don't want to show you is the one you need to see. See them all. I usually hired an inspector to check all the units and I only looked at a couple of the units myself to get an idea of what they looked like inside.

After you see the inspection results, either ask the seller to fix the problems or ask them to lower the price so you can fix the problems.

LEAD-BASED PAINT

The seller will need to certify they don't know anything about lead-based paint problems. If you buy a place built before 1980, you may end up dealing with lead-based paint issues. If you do, remodeling and repairs can become very expensive.

EXISTING LEASES

Ask the seller to provide you with all the rental agreements. This will give you a chance to see all the terms of the leases.

If the leases all expire the month after you get the place, that could be a problem. Read entirely all of the existing agreements so you know what the tenants you are inheriting have agreed to do.

TITLE INSURANCE

Always ask for the seller to pay for title insurance. This is proof that there are no other claims or liens on the property and the seller is legally able to sell the property. You don't want to buy something only to find you are now responsible for four years of back property taxes, or a non-paid construction loan on the recent remodel, or that the seller is not the owner of the property.

TIME IS OF THE ESSENCE

Be sure you do not give the seller a long time to make a decision. Your offer should have an expiration date of three days or less. If you give them too much time, they can wait for better offers. If you make an offer on Friday, have it expire on Sunday night. Then anyone who was going to make an offer on Monday is shut out.

ADDENDUMS

If something was not covered in the main offer, add it as an addendum. List what you want here, such as the terms of a seller-carry loan. List all the personal property you want.

PRESENT THE OFFER TO THE SELLER

Once you have an offer drawn up, present it to the seller. There are two ways to do this. You can either give it to your real estate agent to pass along, or you can present the offer in person yourself.

If the offer is very straightforward, just give it to an agent to present. If you will be making an unusual offer or have something in mind for financing that is not the conventional loan with a bank, you should make the offer in person. The reason for this is one or both of the agents may not understand the offer like you do. Also, if something is unusual, the seller will be more comfortable if they have met you. Character matters.

When you have something out of the norm like owner carry, one of the most important pieces of the puzzle for the owner is your personality. They need to trust you. If you are only a name on a piece of paper, they will often say no. If they meet you in person and you are nice and seem trustworthy, they are more likely to do the deal.

I have had people say they were not interested in seller financing. Then, after they met me, I seemed like a good risk to them and they were interested. When they understood I was a physician, had a good income, and was a responsible person, they also felt better about carrying the mortgage. If you do not present well in person for whatever reason, you are best just sending the papers through and staying out of the loop.

AVOID THE COUNTEROFFER BATTLE

Try to avoid getting into a counteroffer war. If you are not in alignment, ask to talk with the seller about the issue so you can come up with an offer that could be put in writing and accepted. Too many back-and-forth offers also waste time. Think of it like texting. If the issue can be solved with two or three texts back and forth, then it is OK. If it will take more than that and the texts are getting long, picking up the phone and having a conversation will save both of you a lot of time.

AFTER ACCEPTANCE: ESCROW

Once you both have reached agreement and everything is signed, the property will go into escrow. Then you need to rapidly begin your due diligence and get your financing, inspections, and insurance set up. Don't miss any deadlines. They are very important.

Being in escrow is not the same as buying a property. That is why you have all those contingencies in there. If something is not to your liking during this due diligence period, you want to be able to walk away. Many deals fall apart at this step.

BEFORE CLOSING

When it comes time to close, ask the escrow agent to send you all the closing documents one week ahead of time so you can read them before the close. Read every page. Look for errors.

I have found errors on every real estate deal I've made. Escrow officers are people too.

You will not have time to read all 50 pages on the day of signing. You should have read it all ahead of time and had time to make any needed corrections.

Never walk into a closing without reading everything beforehand.

Be sure you do a walk-through the day before you are to close. You want to know everything is as it should be. If they were supposed to evict a tenant before the close, be sure the tenant is gone. If they were supposed to get rid of a pile of garbage in the backyard, be sure the garbage is gone. If you do not do this and close anyway, now you have to deal with something you had negotiated for the seller to correct.

You will need to have the funds in escrow the day before the close, using either a wire transfer or cashier's check.

AFTER CLOSING

You will not get the property after signing the papers. The escrow agent will need to get the money banked, have both parties sign everything, then go to the courthouse and file the papers transferring ownership to you. Then you can have the keys.

If there is anything you think needs re-keying, do it right then, such as an office or supply room. Send a note to all the tenants telling them you are the new owner and how they should handle their rent payments and maintenance needs in the future.

Then go out and celebrate your new purchase. This was a big deal and will change your future. Have a celebration of some sort every time you get another piece of property that moves you one step closer to financial freedom.

"Ninety percent of all millionaires become so through owning real estate. More money has been made in real estate than in all industrial investments combined. The wise young man or wage earner of today invests his money in real estate."

— Andrew Carnegie

Chapter 10

TIPS AND TRICKS TO MANAGING REAL ESTATE FOR BUSY PROFESSIONALS

The most common question I am asked when people find out I managed my own real estate while I was a full-time general surgeon is, "How could you possibly do that? General surgery is a full-time job. You can't fit a second full-time job into your schedule."

The thing is, managing real estate is not a full-time job. In fact, if you want, it could barely be classified as a part-time job or even a job at all. The amount of work you put in is totally up to you.

YOU DON'T HAVE TO DO *EVERYTHING*

Almost every doctor has an office to run. I'd like you to think about a doctor's office for a moment.

When the phone rings, is it the doctor who answers? Not likely. Most offices have a receptionist to handle that job.

When a patient needs to be put in a room, does the doctor do that? No, usually a nurse will do that.

When a patient gets booked for a procedure, is it the doctor who is setting up all the details and going over all the paperwork? Not likely—an office employee will do that.

When a patient has a health insurance issue, is the doctor the one on the phone, on perpetual hold? No.

When you run a doctor's office, even if you own the place, you as the doctor do not do all the tasks it takes to keep the doors open. You have employees to do the various tasks and you have systems in place for them to follow. There is likely a checklist for setting up a procedure and all the forms are preprinted.

In my office, if I said a patient needed a colonoscopy, I wrote it on the back of the billing sheet and handed it to an employee and they took care of everything from there. They had a checklist and a stack of forms. The bowel prep instructions were all preprinted.

You know how to run an office, so why not apply the same principles to your real estate business?

There is no need for you, as the owner of a rental property, to do everything. You do not need to take all the calls or unplug every toilet or approve every new stove. You are a busy professional. You have other important things to do. Set up your real estate to run like your office.

When my wife and I bought our first apartment, we decided to do everything it took to run the place ourselves for one year, as I described in chapter 3. We wanted to learn about everything needed to take care of the property. We did all the room turnovers, cleaning, painting, yard work, screening of tenants, maintenance, accounting, and everything else it took to manage the apartment.

After one year we had a good feel for what it took and began hiring out parts of the business. We also put many systems into place during the first year.

The first job we hired out was landscaping. Eighteen years later, the first person we hired is still taking care of the landscape for all our properties and our home.

Then we hired a maintenance person. Over the years, we've had both small contractors and handymen do this job. During our time handling the maintenance, we set up a system. Urgent calls came straight to the cell phone of either the maintenance person or me. Non-urgent calls went to an answering machine in the office. Once a day the answering machine was checked and the routine maintenance was scheduled.

This is a situation where the old ways are better. I did not want my cell phone ringing for every little thing. We bought an answering machine and hooked it up to a landline with a number only used for this purpose. We then sent a letter to all the tenants and posted it on the property. The letter told them what to do for maintenance. If it was something that needed fixing but didn't need to be done today, like a dripping kitchen sink faucet, then they called the maintenance number and left their information on the answering machine. If it was an emergency such as water running out the neighbor's front door, they had other instructions about where to call. I'll cover emergencies later in this chapter. Overall, the tenants did a good job identifying what things were emergencies and what were not.

Every day, the maintenance person would call in remotely and check for any messages on the maintenance answering machine and schedule a time for repairs to be done. The contractor we had would do the routine stuff on his way to or from his bigger jobs. The handyman would schedule all the maintenance for one day of the week.

My wife and I did not want to be bothered by the routine issues. This system took care of it. No one was calling or texting our cell phones with routine things. During the time we personally managed the 31-unit apartment, we got a true emergency about twice a year. The rest of the calls went to the answering machine.

We set up systems to handle everything, just like the system in my medical office for setting up a colonoscopy. Besides the system for maintenance, we also set up systems for handling appliance repair, flooring replacement, painting, plumbing, and electrical work.

We contacted an appliance store in town. We went in and picked out a stove, dishwasher, refrigerator, and wall air-conditioner unit. If a tenant contacted maintenance for a dishwasher that didn't work, the maintenance person would go by and check it out to see if something simple was missed, like if the breaker was tripped.

If the dishwasher seemed to be the real problem, the maintenance person would contact the appliance store and give them the name, phone number, and address of the tenant and tell them what needed to be fixed. The store had instructions to "fix or replace." They would send a person to check it out and if it could be repaired, they fixed it. If it could not be repaired, they replaced it with the unit we had already picked out. They had our credit card on file and would put the charge on the card and send us the receipt.

The first time I would hear about the problem was when I got the receipt for the repair. The system took care of it without my input. Do you think you could handle that much work for a call about a broken dishwasher? My level of work as the manager was to record the receipt that came in the mail so I could get the tax deduction. And in fact, my wife did that.

For flooring, I went to a local flooring store and picked out a carpet and a vinyl to be used in all the apartments. Just recently, we have switched to a water-resistant laminate flooring that is supposed to last a lot longer than carpet and need less care. If the same flooring is always used, then a repair can be made easily. The same system exists for getting new flooring. The maintenance person looks at the empty apartment when cleaning it up and getting it ready to rent. If the carpet needs replacing, he calls the flooring store and gives the address and they take care of it and send me the receipt. Again, my only involvement as the manager was to record the receipt so I could get a tax write-off.

For paint, we picked out a paint color, Cielo Blanco in semi-gloss, at a local paint store and used it for everything. We bought it in five-gallon buckets. When a bucket was empty we got another one of the same color. Every unit was painted the same color and that made touch-ups easy. Paint is also cheaper in five-gallon buckets. Using semi-gloss makes the walls easier to clean.

By the way, never let a tenant paint the unit, even if they are a painter. Everyone thinks they can paint. A messy paint job that gets paint on the wood trim or cabinets is almost impossible to fix. Don't let the tenants paint.

For electrical and plumbing, we picked one company for each and gave them our billing information. Then when we needed electrical or plumbing work done, it just took a phone call. The maintenance person was to address the issue first and if they couldn't handle it, then they called the professional. Most issues are easy to fix. Changing out a light switch is easy for the maintenance person to do.

Having systems in place to take care of issues automatically will remove the time burden from you as the manager. With a maintenance person and a yard care person and all the systems in place, it took me about 10-15 hours per month to manage the 64 units I owned. That is about the same amount of time I spent in attending church on Sundays.

The only jobs I handled were showing the apartments, selecting tenants, and collecting rent. Even those jobs could have been farmed out, but I wanted something to do besides cashing checks.

Later on, when I started working out of town in locums, I turned everything over to a property management company. Then my job was to oversee their work. I still wanted to have a hand in the place because it was fun and a change of pace for me. So I still have first right of refusal for any big project.

If a tenant leaves an apartment trashed, the property management company calls me first. If I am home and free and feel like doing it, I will go clean up the apartment and do all the repairs and paint. This takes Carolyn and I about three days to do and saves us about $4,000. Sometimes I say I will do it and sometimes I let them do it. Lately we've been traveling so much that I don't really have the time to do this, and I let them handle it. But it's good to know I can do it if I want.

People always want to know how often a tenant leaves an apartment trashed. It does happen, but not much—once every couple of years. It's almost like watching the news. Bad news sells. We will hear about a tornado's destruction for several days, but the news doesn't report all the normal stuff happening every day. Most tenants leave the apartments in good shape and get most of their deposit back. One or two tenants a year cause more damage than the deposit covers. That is less than 3% of tenants. It hasn't been much of an issue, but it does happen.

HOW TO HANDLE VACATIONS

When I was the manager, I needed to get someone to cover if I went away on vacation. I could be the manager if I was home but not from a cruise ship. I had a system set up for that too.

I had a few people who could cover for me during our vacations. One of them was my medical office manager. Whoever covered for me got a list of instructions of who to call for various problems and the key to the apartment office. In the office were all the keys to the apartments so they could gain access to any apartment in an emergency.

I paid them to be available for emergencies while I was gone. Most of the time they did nothing the entire time I was away. Occasionally, they got a call. The extent of their involvement was often to make another call to set up the needed repair. Rarely, they had to actually go to the apartments. I didn't ask them to show the apartment to any prospective tenants. We just didn't show any vacant apartments if we were gone.

AN EXAMPLE OF HANDLING EMERGENCIES

Our emergency system worked as follows: Every tenant had a letter given to them when they moved in, listing emergency procedures. That same letter was posted in the laundry room of each apartment complex.

It stated that in the event of an emergency, they should call the following numbers in order. If no one answered, they were to leave a message with each number and call the next number until they reached a person. Whoever answered would start handling the emergency.

The maintenance person was the first number on the list. Sometimes he was tied up somewhere and so they marched down the list. Our list included the maintenance person, then my home number, then my cell number, my wife's cell number, my father's cell number, and finally my mother's cell number.

Whoever they got ahold of started the ball rolling for the emergency and soon everyone on the list knew what was going on. This only happened a couple of times a year. Let's look at an example.

One real emergency we had was a call from a tenant that water was coming out of an upstairs apartment and running down the stairs. Neither the upstairs nor downstairs tenants were home. I got the call as the first person to answer on the list. (The maintenance person was tied up at the moment.) I went to the apartment, got the keys to the unit, and went inside. I found the inflow pipe to the water heater had broken and water was pouring out of the pipe and onto the floor.

I turned off the water to the water heater by shutting off the valve to that pipe. Then I went to the office and got the wet-dry vacuum and started vacuuming up the water. Before I finished, the maintenance person arrived, having heard the message on his phone, and we both worked to get rid of the water. Then he took over and I left. He replaced the broken pipe and all was well again. Fans were placed in the wet areas and soon everything was back to normal.

This type of thing did not happen very often and when it did, the maintenance person usually took care of it. Sometimes it fell to me or Carolyn.

Once I got a call about a broken toilet. The person got up in the middle of the night and leaned on the back of the toilet and cracked the tank. I got the call at 2 a.m. I told them to turn off the valve behind the toilet and put down towels to soak up the water and someone would be there to fix it in the morning. The maintenance person took care of it in the morning.

SHOWING APARTMENTS

As I mentioned, I showed the apartments and picked the tenants. Initially we would schedule an appointment to show the apartment. We got a lot of no-shows. If they called us on Monday and we scheduled a time on Wednesday to show the apartment when I was free, but they found one they liked on Tuesday, they just didn't show up for the Wednesday appointment. It was no skin off their nose if they didn't show up. They rarely called to tell us they found something else.

We realized that prospective new tenants were urgent issues. It is very expensive to leave a unit empty. A $700-per-month apartment costs $23 per day in lost rent for every day it is vacant. Missing out on a tenant who found another apartment before I showed them mine was costing us money. We changed our tactics.

We made showing the apartment a high priority.

If we got a call on a vacant apartment, we would drop everything to show the apartment right then. Often the prospective tenant was sitting in the car outside the apartment looking at the "For Rent" sign. Either Carolyn, the maintenance person, or I would go right then and show the unit.

We kept our units very clean and the rent was below market value. I knew they would not find a better unit for the price. If they had been looking, they knew that also. If they looked like good prospects and had a clean outfit and a clean car, I gave them an application right then and they usually filled it out on the spot.

We had a small advantage in having Carolyn at home and not working. She was more available in the daytime than I was. If you both work, you can work around that issue. Maybe the maintenance person shows the apartments or you schedule the showing for right after work or on lunch hours. There is always a way to work it out.

SCREENING TENANTS

The only thing I did to check up on tenants, besides looking at how they cared for their car and their clothing, was to call their old landlord—not the one they were currently leaving, who might say anything to get rid of them, but the one before that. A good reference from an old landlord was as good as anything else. Today, I have a property management company who does a background check and credit check and they get the same number of bad tenants as I did with my simplified method.

If the call checked out and they had an income at least three times the rent, then I would meet them at the unit, have them sign the papers and give me a check, and I would give them the keys.

I saved a lot of time showing apartments by qualifying the tenants over the phone before I showed them a unit. I told them we required three times the rent for income and I told them the amount of the deposit. If that was good, I asked them if there were any problems I would encounter with their background and credit check. If they said no, then I showed the apartment. If they said yes, I could usually find out from them the same information I would have received in a credit and background check, but they would tell me for free.

I never charged an application fee. If I did charge one and I turned them down, I was required by law to give them an explanation in writing as to why they were turned down. So not having an application fee saved me time.

EVICTIONS

Evictions are a special case. First, I try to get the tenant to leave by asking nicely. Often they can't leave because they don't have money to leave. I have offered to pay them $100 cash if they would be gone in 24 hours and many took that eagerly. Some said they couldn't move because the person who was going to help them couldn't come. I had the maintenance person bring their truck and move the tenant.

Once I had a worker doing some odd jobs and told him to stop what he was doing and go help the tenant move and do whatever it took to get them out. He came back and told me he had to rent a storage unit for the person. They filled the one they had already rented and still had stuff left to move. So he rented another unit for them and paid for one month. I reimbursed him for the storage unit and the tenant was out.

If the easy way didn't work and I needed to do a formal eviction, I hired that task out through a property management company.

*Be quick to get rid of bad
or nonpaying tenants.*

If you let a bad tenant slide, the other tenants know they can do the same. Treat everyone equally and make them all follow the rules.

A tenant who doesn't have the money to pay the rent this month is unlikely to have enough to pay two month's rent next month. It is hard for them to catch up. I usually talk with them about why they are behind and if the reason makes sense, I work with them. Evictions and room turnovers are expensive. If the reason is bad, then I give them notice to leave unless their rent is paid in full by a certain date. Each state has a time limit for how long they can stay. If they do not leave on time or pay the rent, I start the eviction process. I rarely needed to do an eviction—maybe once every four years. My new property management company is much quicker to evict than I was and they do it about twice a year.

FORMS

There is likely a rental owners association in your area. Sign up with them and you will learn a lot about management and the landlord/tenant laws in your state. The association I belonged to had a monthly newsletter with teaching points and quarterly meetings with guest lectures. They are also likely to have all the proper forms you need to run your real estate business. A 72-hour notice for nonpayment of rent and a 30-day notice to vacate the property for no cause were my most commonly used forms. I made my own rental agreement, but the renters association had one as well. Rental agreements and other forms are also available at most stationary stores.

ADDITIONAL MANAGEMENT TIPS

If you have to do anything more than once, set up a system to automate it. Below are some things I've learned about how to do the important stuff.

HIRING HELP

Try to hire all your workers as 1099 independent contractors. This removes the need to do payroll.

When hiring 1099 independent contractors, you must comply with state and federal laws so your business practices will stand up to an IRS government audit, otherwise you may be responsible for paying certain employment taxes—Social Security at 12.4% and Medicare at 2.8%, currently—for present and past persons determined to be "employees."

You can review the federal guidelines here: https://www.irs. gov/businesses/small-businesses-self-employed/independent-contractor-defined.

"The general rule is an individual is an independent contractor if the payer has the right to control or direct only the result of the work and not what will be done and how it will be done."

The IRS is very specific with these rules for qualifying an independent contractor versus an employee. For example, if you expect a person to work 9 a.m. to noon, Monday, Wednesday, and Friday, that person is an employee. If that person is required to show up to work at a specific time on specific days and do specific things, that person is an employee.

MOVING IN
FIRST MONTH'S RENT AND DEPOSITS

Always collect a full month's rent and security deposit before a tenant moves in. If it is near the end of the month, I collect the last few days of the current month and the full rent for next month. If it is near the beginning of the month, I collect a prorated first month's rent.

Never charge a security deposit equal to the rent, as the tenant will later think they have paid the last month's rent.

Collect a big deposit. You will rarely collect more money from the tenant than their deposit. If they do more damage than the deposit, you will not likely recover your costs.

If you allow pets, collect an extra pet deposit and consider raising the rent for the pet. Pets will often do damage. I've had pets ruin brand-new carpet by peeing all over it. That is a $1,500 loss.

SHOWING AND TURNOVERS

Never show a prospective tenant an apartment that is not ready to rent. Most people cannot imagine what the apartment will look like after it is put back together. Don't lose a prospective tenant thinking you are saving time by showing the apartment before the cleanup is complete.

Advertise the apartments before they are empty. Give the date you expect the apartment to be ready and don't show it before it is ready. You can often get tenants to rent from you even before the unit is cleaned. They have given their 30-day notice to move and they need to know where they are going.

If vacancy rates are high in your area, offer incentives for people to choose your units. Giving a new tenant an inexpensive item such as a new TV or microwave with their move-in or $100 off their security deposit may sway them to your place over the competition. Giving a security deposit break as a bonus sounds great to the tenant—it sounds like they are getting $100. But the security deposit belongs to them anyway so the incentive is their own money. If an incentive will fill the empty apartment four days sooner, you made money on the deal.

DURING OCCUPANCY
ALWAYS PROVIDE GARBAGE SERVICE

Always provide garbage service, even in single-family homes. If you don't, the tenant will save money by dumping the garbage in the backyard and not paying for the garbage pickup service. That is terrible to clean up when they leave.

CHOOSING APPLIANCES

Don't use expensive appliances in rentals. An $800 stove will not bring in more rent than a $400 stove. Tenants don't notice the difference. They also will not take care of the stove like you would. Let them damage a cheap stove.

As you can see, managing the property yourself is not that hard. You will start with only one property and build from there. Every time you do something, set up a system for it to be done automatically next time. When you add a second property, those systems are already in place so each new property is easier to add than the last one. Apartments are easier to manage than single-family homes.

If you treat the property management like you run your business office—delegate and set up systems—you will find you can manage the rentals easily with very minimal time. After I turned over all my property to a property management company, I noticed the owner of that company never left his office.

He didn't answer the phones or do any maintenance or show any property. I realized he was doing the same thing I did. Management was pretty easy for him also.

MAINTENANCE AND REPAIR

During the year we managed our first apartment building ourselves, I learned and put systems in place to make my life easier and the management hours fewer. Now I'd like to share with you some tips on maintenance and repair that will do the same.

Most of you will never choose to do the maintenance on your real estate investments. That's OK. I did it because I liked it. It was fun for me. It also reminded me of my childhood when I helped Grandma and Grandpa work on their properties, and they were projects my wife and I could do together and served as a nice change of pace from surgery.

If you will be hiring out all the maintenance or using a property management company, do not skip this section. You will need to keep an eye on the people who are doing the maintenance. Never let anyone else be totally in charge of any of your investments. You should always be looking over their shoulder. If for no other reason, do it so they know you are looking. This section will help you know what to look for.

KEEP A LOG

We kept a log of all the maintenance we did. We used a spiral notebook and left a few pages for each unit and wrote down anything we had to fix. It will help you see patterns. For example, if this is the fourth time you have had to unclog a toilet, then either something is wrong (i.e., there is something stuck in the toilet), or the tenant is using it improperly.

ANNUAL SAFETY INSPECTIONS

Take a look in every apartment once a year. You can check them all at once or when you go fix something. Inform the tenant in writing that you will be coming. Your state will have a law about how much notice the tenant needs. Then go look around. You are officially looking for smoke detector function and water leaks under the sinks and at the water heater. You are also looking for abuse of the property and illegal activity.

FIX WHAT YOU FIND, BUT CHARGE THEM FIRST

If you find any issues on your inspection, fix them. This is a preventative maintenance issue. If you find they have damaged things, then you should address those as well. If they have punched holes in the walls or broken doors, send them a bill and collect the money before you do the repair work. If you fix it first and then bill them, you will often struggle to collect the money.

CARPETS CAN ALMOST ALWAYS BE CLEANED, EXCEPT FOR BAD PET ODOR

I have taken issue with my property management company as they always want to replace the carpets. Most dirty carpets can be cleaned. They inform me the carpet needs replacing and I go check it myself and about 75% of the time I tell them to keep the carpet and have it cleaned.

Frayed edges of the carpet can often be repaired by stretching the carpet. Just because there is a stain in the carpet doesn't mean you need to replace it. If you stained your own carpet, would you replace it or put a throw rug over the stain?

If you use the same carpet everywhere, you can save some pieces for repair work. If you don't have a match to the carpet, you can steal a piece from the back of a closet and make the repair, then the almost matching piece will be hidden in the closet.

DEALING WITH MOLD

Mold is a touchy subject. Mold is universal in the bathroom. Tenants need to be taught to run the bathroom fan for 30 minutes after a shower. They tend to take a hot shower, cover the walls with condensation, turn off the fan, and run to work. Then mold grows.

Most mold will not come off with standard cleaner. You need one specifically designed for mold and mildew. Bleach also works. Just spray it on and the mold melts away and can be wiped clean. I have been told the mold on the bathroom ceiling is under the paint and won't come off. Then I come in with the spray and squirt it and the ceiling looks like new.

If you see mold, there must be water. If the mold is where water is normally found, like the bathroom, that is normal. If the mold is not where water is normally found, like the living room, you need to look for a water leak. You could have a roof leak, a pipe leaking in the wall, clogged and overflowing gutters, or a broken window seal where rain is getting in.

If you clean up the mold but don't find the water source, it will come back. Be aware that mold could also be inside the walls. If you clean it up but it comes back where water shouldn't be, check between the walls. If it's between the walls, you will likely need to call a professional to clean it up. Expect to spend a lot of money for that—yet another reason to always fix any water leak as soon as you find it.

PAINT IS AN EXPENSIVE ISSUE

I paint everything the same color, Cielo Blanco, and use a latex semi-gloss. This is an easy-to-clean paint. Most marks will wipe off. Touch-ups are easy because I have leftover paint. If you do not have a color match, usually because the place hasn't been painted since you bought it, then you can take a piece of the color to the paint store and they can easily make a match for you.

Be very attentive to how nail holes are fixed. The putty should be applied with your finger and wiped off so only the hole has putty in it. Never fix it with a putty knife. This will leave a one-inch blotch on the wall and require the entire wall to be repainted and you will still see the putty sites. If you fix nail holes correctly, you often don't need to repaint.

Never let the tenant fix nail holes in the walls. I tell them I will fix the nail holes for free. If they use a putty knife, I'm committed to repainting. Many of them fill the holes with white toothpaste, which is not the right thing to do either.

MOST REPAIRS ARE MINOR AND CAN BE FIXED ON YOUR WAY HOME FROM WORK

Most repairs are very easy to fix. They are the same little things you fix at home. If you are at all handy, you can make repairs at the apartments the same way you make them at home. The exact same things break. Just swing by on the way to or from work and fix it. I did a lot of 10-minute jobs that way.

KEEP FREQUENTLY USED PARTS ON HAND

Toilet parts, faucet washers, mold spray, and stove drip pans will get used a lot, so keep them on hand. When I buy a toilet flapper valve, I buy ten of them. Then when I need one, it's sitting there in the office and I don't need to go to the store. Keep track of the parts you use frequently and buy extras.

One of the apartments we bought had a small extra building for storage. We kept our extra parts there. You could put a big shelf in your garage to keep extra parts. One friend drove a pickup and modified the bed to hold extra parts. It is crucial to have a place to store parts if you will be doing the management yourself. Your maintenance person will also need access to these parts.

GARBAGE DISPOSAL TOOL

The most common tool I use to fix a garbage disposal is a pry bar. I keep one handy. People will get things like pennies in the disposal, which get stuck. Turn off the switch and stick the bar in the hole and turn the grinder at the bottom of the disposal, then the penny pops free and you can take it out. Often this can also be done with an Allen wrench used under the garbage disposal to turn the grinder.

Reach in with a tool and not your hand to remove the penny. I found a long spoon and a knife make great garbage disposal tweezers.

And don't forget that most garbage disposals have a reset switch on the bottom. If you turn it on and hear a hum, it is stuck. If you turn it on and don't hear a hum, look for the reset switch on the bottom and push the reset button back in.

YOU CAN GOOGLE AND YOUTUBE ALMOST ALL REPAIRS

Instructions on how to do almost any repair can be found on the internet. I also have a *Reader's Digest* home repair book. You will find that once you know the secret, the repair is easy.

I was helping my son fix up his first rental house. One of the windows was off track and I couldn't figure out how to fix it. I know it must be simple so I looked on YouTube. The answer was a little lever that was partially hidden in the side. Once you flipped that, the window came out and was easy to put back on track. I saved both time and money by not needing to call for professional help.

NEVER IGNORE A WATER LEAK

Never ignore a water leak. Major problems are caused by water. It is much cheaper to fix the leak than to replace all the flooring damaged by the leak. See my prior comments on mold.

WATCH THE PROFESSIONALS AND LEARN WHAT THEY DO

Sometimes you can't figure out how to fix something. That's when you call a professional. If it seems like something you should have been able to do, then watch how they do it and you will be able to do it next time. They might use a special tool and that is the secret. If so, you need to decide if you want to own the tool or call the professional.

A good example is the water heater element. It takes a special large socket to remove and replace that part. If you don't have that, you need to replace the water heater entirely or call a plumber to make the repair. I found the tool in a pawn shop and replaced my own water heater elements. Water heaters have two elements and two controllers to regulate them. If one goes bad, just replace it rather than the entire water heater. If the water heater is 15 years old, bite the bullet and replace the whole thing before the bottom rusts out and causes even more trouble.

OWN A UTILITY TRAILER

A utility trailer is a very handy item for a landlord. There are times you will need to haul something. Someone may leave a bunch of stuff behind when they move out and you can throw it into the trailer and take it to the dump. I have one property with lots of oak trees. Every fall I park the trailer there and hire a teenager to fill it with leaves.

A WET/DRY SHOP VACUUM IS VERY HANDY

This is another indispensable tool. Whenever there is a water leak, I use this to clean it up. It can also come in handy for unclogging toilets. If the plunger doesn't work, the shop vac usually will. Be sure you have one with a three-to-four-inch diameter hose that will wedge into the bottom of the toilet, then turn it on. Just be careful how you empty it. I usually pour the contents back into the toilet when it is working again.

MOST ELECTRICAL STUFF IS SIMPLE

Some people are very uneasy working around electricity. If that is you, just call the electrician. However, if you are comfortable with it, most electrical problems are easy to fix. Putting in a new light fixture or light switch is one of those. Always be sure the breaker is off for that circuit. Some states don't allow an owner to do their own electrical repairs.

MOST PLUMBING ISSUES ARE EASY TO FIX

Plumbing is another thing that seems daunting but is often easy. Replacing washers in dripping faucets, tightening pipe connections under the sink, and running a snake down a clogged drain are all straightforward. Those account for the majority of plumbing issues. If I can't solve it, then I call the plumber.

MOVING OUT
KEEP EXTRA DOORKNOBS AND KEYS

When someone moves out, you will need to change the locks. Many people call a locksmith to come out and do that, which is spendy and takes time. We kept three extra sets of doorknob/deadbolt sets. When someone moved out, we just swapped the parts and the door was rekeyed. That old doorknob will end up on someone else's door after three more people move out.

We also have extra keys made. Then if someone loses their keys, we go into the office and get them a new one. Cost of the key is about a dollar, and we charge them $25 for a key replacement. Keep spare mailbox keys as well.

DON'T DO THE CLEANING YOURSELF

There are lots of people who will clean houses. They are fast and inexpensive. Find one or two you like and bring them in for the final cleaning after a unit turnover. They will do it better, faster, and cheaper than you can do it yourself. They are also happy to get the work.

30 DAYS TO ACCOUNT FOR DEPOSIT

In Oregon, we have 30 days from when the tenant turns in the keys to get them an accounting of their security deposit. Get the work done quickly so you can get them their deposit. If the work will take longer, you can send them a preliminary security deposit accounting before the 30 days and send the final one later. Check your state regulations for the time limits on this.

GET REPAIRS DONE QUICKLY

Having a unit vacant is expensive. Apartment turnovers after a move-out must be done quickly. Once, a tenant moved out and told me the tub wouldn't drain. I couldn't fix it so I called the plumber. The plumber said the pipes under the concrete slab were broken.

That was a big deal. The concrete had to be jackhammered out and the pipes dug out. Then the plumber could fix them and the floors needed to be cemented again.

The plumber told me we needed a demolition crew to take out the concrete, but they didn't think they could get one for at least two weeks. Then they would need to repair the hole and that might take another two weeks to schedule. It would cost $4,000 for the work, not counting the plumber's charges and the one-month vacancy.

You may consider this going above and beyond, but I rented a jackhammer and Carolyn and I uncovered the pipes the next day. Then the plumber did his work. Then Carolyn and I poured the concrete. Then we got the flooring company in to replace the vinyl. The project was done in about six days. Had we not done it ourselves, the apartment would have been empty for an extra month, awaiting this repair.

Turns out running a jackhammer was a pretty easy job. It seemed a little intimidating at first, and it required a little muscle work. After doing a bit of YouTube research, I took some preemptive ibuprofen and tackled the job. I knew if it turned out I couldn't do the job, we could always wait on the demolition team. It cost us less than $100 to rent a jackhammer and buy the concrete. We saved $4,000 in construction fees and a month of vacancy.

I hope these little tips will make maintenance seem less intimidating. If you usually fix stuff that breaks around your own house, you can fix it at the apartment. If you are not at all handy at home, you will be unhandy at the apartment and will be better off hiring it out.

TIPS FOR THE RELUCTANT LANDLORD

You may have started out on the wrong foot in real estate, as a reluctant landlord. Perhaps you had to move but couldn't sell a house and now are renting it rather than selling it for a loss. Here are some ways to improve your situation.

RAISE THE RENT

A negative cash flow is often a big problem for the reluctant landlord. Usually the house was not purchased to be a rental and suddenly it is for rent. If you are not in the real estate business, you might not even know what the going rate for rent might be. You might have found someone and just put them in the place quickly, without assessing the true rental value. If your rent is too low, then raise the rent.

If you want to keep your current tenant, you shouldn't raise the rent more than $25, and not more than once a year. That is considered a nuisance increase. More than that and they might consider moving.

If what you are charging is way off current rates, you can either increase it to current rent levels or ask the tenant to leave and get a new tenant at the new level.

REFINANCE

It might be possible to refinance the property and lower the mortgage payments, thus improving your cash flow. If you think the situation is short term, you might consider an adjustable rate mortgage. This is a bit dangerous, as you may be worse off if the rates increase. Changing the terms of the loan might help. If you move from a 15-year loan to a 30-year loan, the lower payments could make the difference.

MANAGE IT YOURSELF

Managing the property yourself will save you about 10% of the rent rate. But you usually need to live close to the property to do this. Management is pretty easy, but not from a distance.

DO YOUR OWN REPAIRS

You can save thousands of dollars if you are willing to do the major repairs that come up. Doing the room turnovers and the painting, if you are able, can save a lot.

PAY OFF OR PAY DOWN THE LOAN

If you can pay off the loan, you will move to a large positive cash flow. If you can't afford to do that, putting more money into it during a refinance to reduce the borrowed amount could be just enough to make it positive.

CUT YOUR LOSSES

Sometimes remaining a reluctant landlord is not worth the anguish. There is a time to cut and run. Sell the property and take the loss and use it as a deduction on your taxes. I know several people who did this. It is painful, but often the relief of not having what you perceive as a millstone around your neck pays big dividends.

One friend moved away from an area and couldn't sell her house. The area was depressed by the closing of a big factory. She held onto the house for a long time with a negative cash flow. The losses were adding up and there was no end in sight for the local bad economy. She decided she wanted out and sold the property for a loss. That stopped the monthly negative cash flow and capped her loss. She felt so much better once the property was gone.

If you see the possibility of a turnaround in the price, you might consider waiting it out. If that doesn't seem likely, you might as well cut your losses and move on with a lesson learned. Every move doesn't have to make money and a loss now and then will not sink you.

It is better to have one big cut you can heal from rather than dying a death of a thousand cuts.

AVOID THIS SITUATION IN THE FUTURE

The best choice is to avoid becoming a reluctant landlord. You can lessen the chances by never buying a house when you move to an area for a new job. Rent at first and be sure you really like the job and the town and will be staying long term.

Resident physicians should never buy a house. That is a period of your life when renting makes the most sense. The percentage of residents who end up as reluctant landlords is too high. Don't take the risk. I didn't buy my first house until I was an attending. I was financially independent by age 50, and I didn't need to buy a house as a resident to do that. There is no shame in renting. There is a season for everything. Residency is the season for renting.

Chapter 11

THE PROS AND CONS OF PROPERTY MANAGEMENT COMPANIES

SHOULD YOU USE A PROPERTY MANAGEMENT COMPANY?

I've already shown my hand about my preferences in managing the property yourself. It is not very difficult and takes very little time. However you will need to learn the ropes and set up some systems if you want to manage your first property.

Not everyone will believe me about the ease of doing it yourself and will want someone else to do that task. There are situations where the right choice is to hire a property management company. The majority will probably make this choice.

TOO BUSY RIGHT NOW

There are definitely times in our lives when adding one more thing is not good. If you are in one of those times, you will not want a new task added to your plate. You might be studying for a board exam, just had a new baby, were recently diagnosed with cancer, or a parent had a stroke.

If this is one of those times, you will benefit by handing the property over to a manager and stepping back to take care of your life. I have a friend who bought an apartment and the close of escrow kept getting postponed. The eventual closing happened during the holidays and she had big travel plans. That was not a good time for her to start the care and feeding of a new project.

The property was already being managed by a property management company for the prior owner. She asked the management company to keep on doing their thing for awhile. Her plan was to take over the management eventually, when her life slowed down.

The property management company knew the property was coming off their books, but this delayed that event and allowed them to make some more money before it happened, so they were happy to do it.

DON'T THINK YOU CAN DO IT

Many busy professionals are not sure they can manage a property. They have never done it before. They are very confident in what they do professionally but real estate is a scary new adventure.

I guarantee managing a property is much easier than what it took to get to your current position professionally. But if you don't think you can do it, you are probably right.

Maybe you just can't do it yet. Over time, as a real estate investor, you will grow more confident.

TRAVELING

If you are semi-retired or retired and traveling a lot, I do not recommend managing your own property. You would have thought after I retired from my practice I would have more time to manage my property. The opposite was true. When I retired from my practice, I started traveling. As I write this, I am snowbirding in Arizona and Southern California.

I don't recommend managing property from afar, and especially not your first property.

I have a friend who manages several properties. Every summer, he hops in his motorhome and travels across the country for several months. He is the manager of the property, but he has an onsite team to place tenants and do the maintenance. He just has his business phone forwarded to his cell phone and answers the phone as if he is still home. Most people never know he is 2,000 miles away. He has enough systems and people in place that he can manage from afar. He also has been doing it for a long time.

DON'T FEEL YOU ARE "HANDY" ENOUGH

After the "not enough time" excuse, the next one I hear most often is, "I'm not handy enough to do this." Certainly there are people who don't know which end of a wrench to use, but most busy professionals can do 80% of the maintenance work needed for their property.

At one point, I hired my father to do the maintenance on my properties. He had retired from his job and needed something to do. His initial thought was, "I don't know how to do that."

I pointed out that he fixed most things at his own house. I asked him if he could change a light switch if it was bad. He said yes. I asked him if he could replace a flapper valve in a toilet tank. He said yes. I asked him if he could replace a broken doorknob. Yes, he could.

I asked him if he could do all that at his own house, why couldn't he do those things at my apartments? He thought he could. So he took the job. He found that he indeed could fix most of the issues that came up. If he didn't know how, he had permission to call a professional. He would then watch the professional and see if he could learn to do it himself next time. Every time he did it himself, he saved me a lot of money.

He went on to do that job for about 10 years. Most people are intimidated by the unknown. Dad had never been the mainte-nance person for 64 rental units before. He didn't know if he could do it. Turned out he could do it just fine. So can you, if you want to.

WANT THE CASH FLOW TO BE COMPLETELY PASSIVE

Some people really want their real estate cash flow to be truly passive. When I retired and began to travel, I felt that way too. There is nothing wrong with wanting it to be 100% passive. You can run your rental exactly like a real estate syndication or REIT (Real Estate Investment Trust) would be run—someone else will do everything and you will just cash the checks. As the owner, you have the opportunity to make it as passive as you want it to be.

DON'T WANT TO PUT IN THE TIME TO LEARN THE ROPES

Like any new endeavor, there will be a learning curve. Some people don't want to go through that curve. Some people feel they already have one job and don't want another. For those people, there are property management companies to fill the gap.

YOU CAN EASE INTO IT AND HAVE THE MANAGER COVER SOME PARTS

If only parts of the process are not appealing to you, you can do what you want and have a property management company do the rest. I didn't want to do evictions or even learn how, so I hired the management company to do that. You can also hire them to do all the tenant placements and screening. They will likely do any of the parts you don't want to do. They are there to make a living and if you hire them, it serves their purpose.

If you would like to manage your property but are intimidated by the thought, you could have a management company manage the first one and follow what they do. Then when you buy the second one, you could manage that one. Eventually you can either take over all of them, none of them, or just the ones you want to manage.

My wife liked showing the apartments in a complex for ages 55-plus. She did not like showing to younger people. She would have been happy with us managing the senior apartments and giving the property management company the other apartments to manage. You are the owner, so you can do what you want and farm out what you don't want.

THE BENEFITS OF HIRING A PROPERTY MANAGEMENT COMPANY

There are some definite advantages to hiring a property management company. Let's cover a few of them.

SYSTEMS ARE IN PLACE

You will not likely be the first client of the property management company. That means on day one, they already have all the systems in place to smoothly take care of your property. You will hit the ground running.

KNOWLEDGE OF LANDLORD/TENANT LAWS

They have been doing this for a while and keep up with all the landlord/tenant laws and the changes that come about. My property management company recently sent me emails to update me on some important legislation as it was happening in the state capital. You are not likely to come afoul of the law with anything they do.

FORMS

When you first start, you will not even be aware of all the forms you will need to use. When I became a member of the local rental owners association, I saw the list of the forms they sell. There were so many and most of them I have never needed. The management company will already have all the forms and know about their proper use.

NECESSARY STAFF

They will likely have plenty of staff to cover your needs, from showing the apartments to collecting rent to doing repairs. You will not need to find any people to do your work.

SUPERVISE SUBCONTRACTORS

When a subcontractor must be brought in for bigger repair jobs, the property management company will follow up with the subcontractors and check their work. They will see that everything is finished properly.

I once had a tenant drive their car into the wall of a unit. The unit was uninhabitable because the impact moved the outside wall, the stairs, and an inside weight-bearing wall. I was out of town and the property management company took care of getting the property repaired.

OFFICE

This can be a real benefit—an actual place for tenants to go when they need something. I do not give out my home address to the tenants and I do not have a business office for the property. A management office also makes showing an apartment easier. Prospective tenants come to the office, check out a key, and go look at the place themselves.

CAN HANDLE MORE THAN ONE UNIT TURNOVER AT A TIME

Sometimes more than one apartment will become vacant at the same time. I had only one maintenance person and he couldn't fix both apartments at the same time. That lengthened vacancy times. The management companies will be able to turn over rooms faster, which saves money on vacancies.

AVAILABLE 24/7/365

You will not need to worry about vacation coverage. The management company will make arrangements for the property to be covered for emergencies. The 2 a.m. call will not come to your phone.

GOOD ACCOUNTING SYSTEMS

They will take care of the accounting and saving receipts. They can turn in the results to your CPA for taxes.

THE DISADVANTAGES OF HIRING A PROPERTY MANAGEMENT COMPANY

Like everything else in life, there are also disadvantages to using a property management company. Here are a few.

MORE EXPENSIVE

You will have to pay them. Depending on your area, you may pay 5-10% of gross rents. That is only to have them working for you. Then you will pay additional money if they need to do anything like evictions, placements, and maintenance. Maintenance charges will be higher with them than if you did it yourself. You do have to offset their cost with the time you would need to do the same job.

Most people don't realize they are paying these same fees if they use a REIT or syndication. They just don't see the charges as they get buried in the paperwork.

IT'S NOT THEIR MONEY

It is much easier to spend other people's money than to spend your own. Since the management company is not the owner, they will spend more freely than you would. They will also not make the same decisions as you. I struggled with that after doing my own management for 12 years. They did things differently than I would. I had to let that go.

THEY MANAGE OTHER PROPERTIES IN ADDITION TO YOURS

When someone calls me to see my property, I only show them my property. When they contact the property management company to see my property, they may show them other similar properties as well. I could miss out on a tenant that way. Likewise, if there are several vacancies in their inventory, they might not be able to get to yours for a while since they have others to deal with also. You are not their only client.

EASIER FOR THEM TO REPLACE THAN FIX

They will be quicker to replace things than to fix them. Replacing is faster and they can get on with other issues. Fixing might be cheaper for you, but slower for them.

NOT FLEXIBLE

Their employees need to follow the company rules. They won't talk to Mrs. Smith about why her rent is late—they will just send a late rent notice. If Mrs. Smith doesn't respond, they will start eviction proceedings. I pay about four times more in eviction expenses with a property manager compared to when I was able to speak to the tenant and make arrangements.

TENANTS DON'T LIKE THEM

I heard a lot of grumbling from tenants when I switched over to the property management company. I gave much more personal service than the management company does. Tenants prefer being treated like people and not like "the tenant at 516C A St." Tenants also thought they got quicker service and responses to their calls when the owner was involved.

THEY CAN'T MAKE EXTRA MORTGAGE PAYMENTS

If you are trying to pay down your debt, the management company will not be able to make extra payments for you. They can handle a regular mortgage payment every month, usually for a small additional fee. You will need to make the extra payments yourself.

QUICK TO EVICT

I already mentioned my eviction rate is higher with the management company. Since they get paid to do the eviction, they are biased toward quick moves. So they will start eviction processes a few days after the rent is late. As I mentioned earlier, I was evicting every few years, while they are evicting every few months.

THEY ARE NOT IN THE BUSINESS OF SAVING YOU MONEY

There was a noticeable difference in the money spent on repairs from when my father was the maintenance person to when the property management company was in charge. My father was always trying to save me money. That is not the priority of the management company.

PROSPECTIVE TENANTS CAN'T SEE APARTMENTS AFTER HOURS

I did lose some prospective tenants by not being able to show them an apartment after hours. The property management company closes at 5 p.m. and is not open on the weekends. No apartments get shown after 5 p.m. or on weekends. I'm sure I lose more prospective tenants to the places run by an owner who will show them the apartment after dinner. But this could be offset by their availability all the time during the day.

Overall I have had a positive experience with my property management company. There are the pluses and minuses but the ability for me to travel the world now and not worry about the real estate is great. As long as I was home working, I didn't need that luxury. Now I am out of town 50% of the time and the property management company is very helpful.

"Risk comes from not knowing what you're doing."

— Warren Buffett

Chapter 12

BUYING ONE PROPERTY PER YEAR IS A GREAT RETIREMENT PLAN

In our current have-it-all-now society, no one wants to work their way up to being wealthy. They want it right now. But that is not the way it works. We all have to start at the beginning. No one gets to start in the middle or the end of a journey.

I watched how my grandparents did real estate. My grandfather worked in the mill and would save up some money for a down payment on a small, old house that was a bit run down. He would make a down payment, or sometimes even pay cash for the house. Then a year or three later, he would do it again.

With each additional house, they fixed the problems and then rented it out. They built their real estate portfolio one house at a time. They kept their eyes peeled for bargains and once bought a house for one dollar.

So when we started, I did the same thing. But I didn't buy single-family homes. I did it with small apartment buildings. I bought the first one in 2001 and the fifth and last one in 2007. That was a little less than one apartment building per year.

The first was 31 units in 2001, then eight units in 2002, then four units in 2005, then nine units in 2007 (this was a partnership), and the last one was 12 units in 2007. Then the crash happened in 2008, but it didn't have much effect on us, since we weren't selling.

After we bought the last apartment, my wife felt we had enough to finance our retirement, so there was no need to continue buying more. She wanted to pay off what we had instead of buying more. Without her persuasion, I'm sure I would have just kept buying. After 2008, I could have bought at a great discount and had an even bigger retirement income. But she was right, once you have enough, you can stop playing the game. Otherwise, there is never an end in sight.

HOW MANY IS ENOUGH?

Continuing to buy in perpetuity is not necessary. When you begin your real estate investing, it's helpful to understand what your goals are. Do you want enough to supplement your retirement, cover all your retirement, or make you a billionaire?

Knowing what your end point is before you get started will help you stop when you reach enough.

I didn't set out to buy one property a year; I set out to invest in real estate. I developed some criteria for what I wanted and passed that on to a realtor who was looking for me. It turned out that not many properties came available with my criteria and that kept my pace down.

Had I been looking at single-family homes, there would have been a ton to evaluate. By only looking at small apartments, the number of available units for sale was much smaller. I recommend, as a busy professional, that you concentrate your efforts on small multifamily properties and it will drastically lower the number of units you need to evaluate.

So how did it work out for me? I bought each property that did not have partners with no money down. In 2002, the first full tax year, I had just over $22,000 in cash flow and all of it was tax-free. I put all the cash flow back into the property to pay down the loans. By 2018, the cash flow was over $150,000 with about half of it being tax-free due to depreciation. In addition, the equity had grown to over $3,000,000.

I maxed out my office retirement plans each year until I left the practice after 20 years. I maxed out my IRA until around 2006. I am currently pulling money out of my retirement plans using the 4% rule, which provides about $70,000 per year.

The real estate cash flow is more than double my retirement plan cash flow using the 4% rule. And I invested in real estate for a shorter period of time and put in less money as well.

What would it look like if a person were to buy one property a year as a retirement plan? I set out to see what that example might look like and set it up with small investments like my grandparents did. You may want to start out with single-family homes if that is your comfort zone.

There are many ways you can set up this arbitrary calculation. No money down, 50% down, one house every other year or even every third year. Here are the parameters I used for this example: Buy one single-family home each year for 15 years with 25% down and bank financing at 5% on a 15-year loan. Make no extra payments on the loans and each loan will be paid off in 15 years. Wait 15 years after you buy the last house before you retire so there are no loans left during retirement.

Additional parameters I used for this calculation: You start at age 30 and retire at age 60. Each house will be the same value and will appreciate at 3% per year. So each year, you will pay slightly more to get the same house. Cash flow on the day of purchase is zero for each house, with all the proceeds initially going to cover the 15-year mortgage. Rents increase 3% per year and expenses increase 2% per year. Therefore, cash flow will begin in the second year and continue to increase by 1%

each year. As cash flow starts, it is saved in an investment account that will average 5% return over the 30 years. The first house was below median home price ($226,000) at $150,000 with a $1,500 initial rent.

At the time of retirement, 30 years later, the 15 mortgages are all paid off. The total amount of down payment money invested is $697,459. The total value of the appreciated properties is now $5,461,340. The total value of the cash flow investment account is $3,533,481. Thus the net worth of your 30 years of real estate investing is $8,994,821.

You have a monthly cash flow of $14,556, which is the net operating income. If you withdraw 4% of the $3,533,481 investment account each year, you would add another $11,778 to your monthly cash flow. This means your retirement income is $26,334 per month.

I suspect most readers were lost in all those calculations. It requires quite a spreadsheet to make that all happen and can't really be done in your head. There is too much to put it into a simple chart. Suffice it to say, 15 free-and-clear rental houses will produce a lot of cash flow.

I think that would be a sufficient retirement income, don't you? If not, then just pick up a few more until it is enough. If you were to invest those down payments into an investment account instead of buying property, you would have to average

11% interest to have the equivalent net worth the properties have, which includes the property value and the investment account value. This all excludes any tax effects.

That example was investing in small properties. Imagine if you did the same investing in small apartment complexes one a year, or every other year, for a few years like I did.

So start slow. Just buy one property. Get all the systems set up to make it efficient so it will not use up much of your time. Then you can have your realtor begin looking for the next property. Just keep that up until you reach your goal.

As long as you are still working and bringing in good money from your professional practice, don't take any of the cash flow to spend. Use it all to either pay down the mortgages or purchase more property. After you retire, you can start spending the cash flow.

Use the snowball method to pay off the mortgages. Concentrate on only one mortgage at a time and pay it off, then move to the next. Then when you retire, you can refinance everything that still has a mortgage and live on the cash flow. The refinance should boost the cash flow as I discussed earlier, but you don't need to refinance unless you actually need the added cash flow.

HANDLING MULTIPLE PROPERTIES AND DECIDING WHEN YOU HAVE ENOUGH

I was recently talking with a client who wanted to get into real estate investing. He planned to start with single-family homes, as he was scared of multifamily apartments. I asked him what scared him. He thought they would be harder to manage. After only a little convincing, I was able to show him that one multi-family unit is easier to manage than several single-family units.

If we were to compare eight houses versus one eight-unit apartment complex, this is what we would find: If you needed to check on two units, the houses might be across town from each other, but the apartments units are 50 feet apart. You can have a storeroom on site with spare parts at the apartment. You have all the parts for several units all together. The apartment has only one roof, one yard, one location, one water bill, one electric bill, one insurance bill, one tax bill, and one stop to check on it if need be.

There is an economy of scale with the multi-unit place. The more doors you buy, the less they each cost. But apartments often rent out for the same price as an equivalent-sized house. Management of an apartment is the same as management of a house. The repairs are the same and the problems are the same, but the profit per unit will be higher.

237

You can own eight units with one real estate transaction, but the houses will require going through escrow eight times. You will need to evaluate eight different offers to buy those houses but only one offer for the apartment.

As you can see, there really is nothing scary about the apartment. So why not save on the economies of scale and make more money with less time invested? The more units you own, the more affordable it will be to have a property management company involved.

HOW TO SET GOALS

How will you know when enough is enough? I have heard many people say they were going to start investing and buy until they had 50 houses. Don't set a number of units as your goal—set a certain cash flow as your goal.

In our case, when we stopped buying, we had a cash flow of about $50,000 and NOI of about $225,000. I was 45 years old. It would still be several years before I retired. Since we have continued to pay down the loans and the rents have continued to rise, it only took a few more years before the cash flow surpassed our living expenses, which are about $100,000 a year. That was why Carolyn wanted to stop buying more property. Without adding any more property, the cash flow supported us by the time I was ready to retire.

After the properties are paid off completely, the cash flow will be the NOI. With rents continuing to climb, that will put us over the quarter-million mark. I think we will be able to live on that.

Look at what your expected income needs will be when you retire. Then you can project how much income you want from your real estate investments based on your expenses and other income sources. Once you get started, you will have a better handle on what your properties earn. When you have enough to meet your projection, you can stop adding more.

Chapter 13

TAXING ISSUES

One of the great things about real estate investing is the tax benefits. Using depreciation to offset the cash flow from taxes and the postponing of any capital gains from appreciation makes this investment behave very much like an additional retirement plan. In order to reap these benefits, you need to learn to work with the system. A large part of that is keeping records. Another critical part is working with a good CPA.

KEEPING THE BOOKS AND PREPARING FOR TAXES
HIRE AN ACCOUNTANT

There are many things you can do yourself, but I think the tax accounting should not be one of them. Tax laws change every year and you want to be sure you get all the tax breaks you can. Yes, it is possible for you to do your taxes yourself, but don't. At the peak of my tax return history, I counted 56 interconnected forms that were sent to the IRS. There were several more work-sheets that were not sent. The odds that you can get them all right are not great.

Your accountant will also be able to help you with advice. Don't hire a tax preparer—you need a CPA with good business sense, one who will be aggressive at getting you tax write-offs but will not cross the line into shady areas.

When they have prepared the taxes, go over them yourself. It is a great learning experience and you are the best person to catch errors. The CPA prepares returns for many clients, but your only client is you. You know the information better than the CPA and you will pick up things they cannot see.

A great example was the time we had held an office meeting for my surgical practice to go over the year-end accounting and bonus information with the attorney, the CPA, the partners, and the office manager. All thought it looked good.

I brought the paperwork home and my wife picked it up and immediately said it was wrong. She knew that one particular category should be equal for all the partners. and she noticed they were not equal on the paperwork. No one at the meeting picked that up. It turned out one of the partner numbers was entered in another partner's section. One got zero and the other got double. So check the CPA's work. You know your investment the best.

IT TAKES RECEIPTS TO GET TAX BENEFITS

You are in this business partially for the tax benefits. In order to get them, you need to be diligent about keeping receipts. If you ever get audited, these will come in handy.

I did get audited and we had every piece of backup information the IRS asked for and they were skunked. They thought they could get something but they got nothing. If you think it might be deductible, then keep the receipt. File them in a way you can find them later. We kept all our receipts filed first by category (repairs, water, gas) and then by date. All the expenses were also in an Excel file so we could find the date on the computer and get the needed receipt.

AUTOMATE BILLS

The more you can automate things, the easier your life will be. We automated all the recurring bills. This included water, sewer, garbage, electric, and gas. I already mentioned automating the vendors such as appliance repair and installations and floor coverings earlier.

If you can, automate the mortgage payments as well. Most of our mortgages were with private lenders and those we were unable to automate.

ACCELERATED DEPRECIATION OF APPLIANCES AND FIXTURES

A nice way to accelerate the depreciation is to take all the parts of the property that will not last 27.5 years—appliances, carpets and flooring, and water heaters—and depreciate them faster, thus getting a greater write-off early on. Your CPA will be able to help you with how to do that. This gives you a larger write-off in the early years.

RECORD-KEEPING SYSTEMS

Pick a good computer program you like and track all your income and expenses. If you are using a property management company, they will do this for you. We use Excel and make our own spreadsheets (an advantage of having a wife who was a corporate accountant). Others use Quicken or QuickBooks. I've even seen it tracked by handwritten ledgers.

However you want to do this, it is much easier for your CPA, come tax time, if everything is organized.

Having all your business expenses on one business credit card is another nice record-keeping system.

Whatever you do, don't hand your CPA a shoebox full of receipts at the end of the year. You can do better than that.

TRACK THE VACANCY RATE

Keep track of your vacancy rate. Every time you have an empty unit, write down the total number of days it was vacant. If you track this, it will make it easier to estimate vacancies for any future property you might buy. You will have real data and not estimates.

1099 CONTRACTORS VERSUS W-2 EMPLOYEES

The best way to get help is by using 1099 independent contractors to do all your work. If you do this, you need to send those workers a 1099 before January 31 of the next year. You also need to send the IRS form 1096 along with a copy of the 1099s.

If you hire them as employees, you will need to do payroll and pay payroll taxes. Then you will need to send them a W-2 form by January 31. Your kids are an exception to the employee rule. You do not need to pay them through a payroll system. Hiring your kids to work for you is a great thing to do. You can get the work done and your kids can get the money. Yard work, accounting, cleaning, fixing, and painting are things they can learn to do.

At one point we had our oldest son tallying the rental checks and making the bank deposit slips. We gave him a pile of checks and a list of what rent should have been collected. He compared the checks we received with the list. He set up all the deposit slips and my wife would take that to the bank. He then handed me a list of the tenants whose rent was late.

BUSINESS CHECKING AND SAVINGS ACCOUNTS

Keep your business money separate from your personal money. Open a separate checking account and savings account for your investment real estate. If you only have a few rentals, it can be a personal account. If you have many rentals, you might need to get a business bank account, depending on the bank's rules for number of deposits and withdrawals.

Use a savings account to save money for periodic payments. Every month you should transfer 1/12 of the property tax money and insurance costs into the account if they are not included in your mortgage payment. If you have any balloon payments coming up, be sure to set aside the money needed if you don't plan to refinance them.

Always keep some cash on hand to handle any repairs and vacancies that come up. I like to keep a minimum of two months operating expenses in the checking account. Also any big upcoming repairs should have money set aside to cover the costs. Just be sure you are always ready when bills come.

You should keep the security deposits in their own separate account.

INSURANCE

It is important to have good insurance on the property. The insurance prices will keep going up every year. It can save you money to look into a new insurance company every few years, as prices fluctuate greatly. Always get at least three bids for new insurance.

Check to see if the property is in a flood zone. If you are getting bank financing, they will require flood insurance. If you are getting owner financing, they might not require it, but you should pay for it anyway. You might consider other insurance and riders depending on what type of issues are in your area, such as hurricanes, forest fires, tornados, and earthquakes. Flood insurance is the only extra insurance I have used.

Always remind your tenants to get their own renter's insurance. Your insurance will replace the building, and the tenants' insurance will replace their belongings.

LLC

I think an LLC is the best way to own your real estate. Then if you happen to get sued, they can only go after the business and not you personally. Some people think you should have a separate LLC for every building, but I think that is overkill. That would also mean a separate checking account for every rental, which would be very cumbersome.

We have one LLC that owns all the property and one bank account. That way the income from one property could cover a big expense in another. They don't cross-cover like that on your taxes, but they can with the bank account. Then you only need one emergency fund for the whole business.

BUSINESS MEETINGS

Have a business meeting once a year and record the minutes. If you are the sole owner, you will be the only one present for the meeting, but have it anyway. In my case, my wife was my partner with the LLC so the two of us held the meeting. If you have a bigger partnership, invite everyone and record who attended. Have another business meeting before any big event. If you are buying a building, have a meeting and record in the minutes that permission was given for the purchase of the building. It might be a bit of overkill, but it makes your business look very official.

TENANT RECORDS

When tenants move out, you will give them their security deposit back, minus any charges. Then you should staple all of their information together and keep it forever. You will get calls for references from future landlords. It will be very easy for you to look up the tenant in your file and let the landlord know how they were as tenants when they lived in your properties. You only have to keep this information for seven years, but I keep these longer to help out fellow landlords.

These tips for how to set up your business and how the tax laws apply should give you some basics to get you rolling in the care and feeding of your real estate business. Set it up with the same care you set up your other businesses and it will be smooth sailing.

DEPRECIATION AND ITS EFFECT ON TAXES

When you purchase a property, you will need to split the purchase amount into the value of the land and the value of the improvements or buildings on the land. The improvements are considered temporary and are given 27.5 years of life, so you can deduct about 3.6% of this value against your profit every year. I mentioned this earlier as one of the great benefits of investment property.

HOW TO CALCULATE THE INCOME TAX BENEFITS OF DEPRECIATION

If you buy a property for $800,000 and $150,000 is attributed to the land, then $650,000 can be depreciated. Dividing $650,000 by 27.5 gives you an annual depreciation tax write-off of $23,636.36. So the first $23,636.36 you earn in profit will be tax-free. This deduction will last you for 27.5 years and then will end.

HOW DEPRECIATION AFFECTS CAPITAL GAINS TAXES

After 27.5 years, the buildings and improvements on the property have been fully depreciated. If you were to sell the property at this point, essentially all of the purchase price becomes capital gains profit and is subject to taxes. Your profit will not be the difference between your selling price and the $800,000 you paid for the property. The basis for profit calculation and capital gains tax will be the $150,000 you paid for the land. Because you wrote off the value of the buildings and improvements over the last 27.5 years as depreciation, they will be considered zero value—as if you got them for free.

This is why it is best not to sell, but to 1031 exchange the property for a new one and avoid the capital gains taxes.

If you wish to spend the profit from the sale of your property, you will need to pay the capital gains taxes and then you can spend the rest. If you exchange it, you'll have no money to spend. If you want money from the sale to spend, you can do a partial 1031 exchange and take some of the money and keep the rest in the new property and not pay taxes on that portion.

APPRECIATION

This is another great benefit of investment real estate. Over time, a property tends to increase in value. Those increases in value are not taxed unless you sell. Your 401(k) is treated similarly.

There will be years when the value of the property will go up and years when it will go down. But in the long run, the value tends to increase. Unless you plan to sell, you have no reason to be concerned about its current market value.

It is difficult to establish an accurate property value each year and generally you don't need to. However, since I do track my net worth, I use the county assessor's real market value number from the property tax bill to determine its worth. Over time, this figure usually falls behind the real value.

The important thing to remember is you can hide this appreciation from the IRS and never pay taxes on it if you play the game right.

STEP-UP IN BASIS WITH INHERITANCE

This is one of the best features of the IRS tax code for investment property. The *basis* is what the IRS is using as the purchase value of a property for calculating capital gains on a sale. If you buy a property for $800,000, that is your basis on the day of purchase. Then over time as you take depreciation each year, the basis drops by the depreciation number. So when you sell it, you will owe capital gains on the difference between the current basis and the selling price.

Let's say you started with a basis of $800,000 and over time your depreciation has dropped the basis to $400,000. But the property is now worth $2,000,000. If you sell it for $2,000,000, then your capital gains for taxing purposes will be the difference between the $2,000,000 sales price and the current basis of $400,000. You would owe taxes on $1,600,000 of capital gains.

But what would happen if you died before you could sell the property and your kids inherited that same property? They would get a step-up in basis. They inherit a property worth $2,000,000. That will become their basis. Now, if they were to sell the property for $2,000,000, there would be no capital gains at all because they sold the property for the value of the basis in the property, so the difference between the sales price and the basis was zero. *No taxes owed as a result of the sale.*

If they decide to keep the property, they can start depreciating the property based on the new basis value of $2,000,000, not the $400,000 that was your basis before you died. Your kids get all that capital gains profit without paying any capital gains taxes. This step-up in basis is a way to never pay capital gains taxes on a property if you just keep handing it down to the next generation.

If your estate gets too large, there still may be some estate tax owed, which is different than capital gains taxes.

TAX BENEFITS OF DONATING TO CHARITY

Due to this step-up in basis at your death, it is good for you to either pass the property on to your kids or give the property to charity at the end of your life. Giving it to charity, even when you are still alive, has the same step-up in basis as if you passed it on to your kids. Also, if you give the property to charity while you are still alive, you can deduct its current value as a donation to charity (the $2,000,000 value and not the $400,000 basis). Then you'll never pay taxes on the appreciation and capital gains of the property. It becomes a truly tax-free investment.

If you do choose to give a property to charity, give them the actual property. If you sell the property first, you will then owe capital gains taxes and will have less to give to the charity. If you give them the property, they get it at the current market value and can sell it without paying capital gains taxes. That's a win-win deal for you and the charity. They get the full $2,000,000 from the sale and you get a $2,000,000 tax deduction for something you paid $800,000 to buy.

PROPERTY MORTGAGE INTEREST IS FULLY DEDUCTIBLE

I am often asked if a person should pay off their home mortgage or their rental mortgage first. My answer is always *pay off the home mortgage before the rental.*

The home mortgage is not fully deductible on your taxes. Only the portion of the interest exceeding the standard deduction will be deductible on your home mortgage. But the rental is an investment and is treated differently.

All of the interest is fully deductible on the rental, so take advantage of that and pay it off last.

Also, once your home is paid off, you can't lose it to the bank. If hard times come, it is better to lose an investment property than to lose your home.

HOME OFFICE DEDUCTION

It is acceptable for you to take a deduction for a portion of your home if you use it exclusively as an office for your real estate business.

I have never used this deduction as it complicates the handling of your home, tax wise. When you sell the home, part of it will be treated as your home and part of it will be treated as a business. You might think twice about taking this deduction, but it is available if you want it.

So if 10% of your home was used as an office, and you took a deduction for it every year, then when you sell the house, that 10% will be taxed on the profit the sale made. It messes up the deal of not paying taxes on your home appreciation. Also there are strict rules for declaring the home office space. It really must be a space used only for your work.

WHEN TO HAVE AN EIN

EIN stands for Employer Identification Number. This is the number you use for reporting income taxes if your real estate business issues its own tax return. For most investors, your real estate investments will appear on schedule E of your personal tax return, even if the property is in an LLC.

For tax purposes, if you have your property in an LLC, it will be a disregarded entity. Therefore all the income and expenses will pass through to your personal tax return and you will pay the taxes under your Social Security number.

If you decide to turn your property into a corporation, then your investments will have their own tax return and will need to have an EIN because it will not be using your Social Security number for IRS identity.

If you decide to have employees in your real estate business, then you will need to get an EIN and you will be handling payroll under that tax ID number and not your Social Security number.

WRITING OFF YOUR AUTOMOBILE

One of the great benefits of owning your own business is all the extra tax write-offs. One of them is the ability to write off your vehicle. If you are an employed professional, such as an employed physician, you do not get this benefit. Owning a real estate investment business will get you back into the business of getting write-offs.

First of all, don't fall for the line about how leasing a vehicle is good because you can write it off. Leasing is not a financially good move. Owning is the smart play. Both ways can be written off, so don't use this as an excuse to lease. (In fact, I recommend paying cash for vehicles whenever possible, because paying interest on a vehicle loan is wasted money. Don't fool yourself into thinking it is better to have a loan so you can write off the interest. The interest will cost much more than the deduction. If you paid $100 in interest and your marginal tax rate is 30%, then you will get 30 cents back from the government for every dollar of interest paid. You lose 70 cents in paying interest. I cover this in my book *The Doctors Guide to Eliminating Debt.*)

To write off the vehicle, you need to use it for business purposes, but it can also be for personal use. The business is real estate—buying, selling, and managing. So any miles you drive looking for property, going to the realtor, going to work on the property, checking out a tenant complaint, going to the bank, or anything else you can think of that is real estate oriented can be deducted.

There are two ways to take an automobile deduction: either use the federal mileage allowance or use actual costs. For both of them, you need to keep track of the miles you drive for business. Keep a notepad in the vehicle to record those miles or use a phone app.

For the mileage allowance, you would simply multiply the number of miles you drove for business by that year's federal allowance. For 2019, that is $0.58. This is the simplest way to do it. Keep track of the miles and multiply by that number.

For the actual cost, you need to not only track your miles but also every expense for the vehicle. Then you will calculate the percentage driven for business by dividing the number of business miles by the total number of miles driven that year. Then you will multiply that by the total cost of operating the vehicle.

Business Miles/Total Miles
=
Mileage Ratio

Mileage Ratio x Total Vehicle Expenses
=
Vehicle Write-Off

The latter method is more work, but sometimes it gives you a bigger deduction. The first year, you might figure it both ways and see which gives you the best deduction.

You don't need to buy a new vehicle to benefit from this deduction. Just start writing off the one you are already driving.

EXAMPLE OF A VEHICLE DEDUCTION

I thought I would give you an example of the power of the automobile deductions. This example is based on the rules when I purchased the company SUV. The rules change every year so consult your CPA to maximize this benefit.

I purchased an SUV that had a large towing capacity to pull a heavy trailer owned by my real estate LLC. I traded a car worth $15,000 and bought a car for $36,000. That deal would normally cost the car plus $21,000 cash. That is not how it worked out for me.

I entered the dealer ready to pay $36,000 cash for the new car. They offered me 0% financing for 36 months. I realized I was paying 8% on a property loan with almost the same value. I decided to take the 0% loan, and I used my cash to pay off the 8% real estate loan.

Using the $36,000 to pay off the 8% loan saved me $4,612 in interest, when amortized over the three years of the car loan.

We kept track of the mileage driven and only used this vehicle for real estate driving. Since it did occasionally get used for personal miles, it calculated out to a 95% business use for 5,000 miles driven. That meant the business miles totaled 4,750. At that time the government was allowing 37.5 cents per mile deduction (4,750 x 0.375 = $1,781 deduction). My marginal tax rate at the time was 28% federal and 9% state for a total of 37%. So that's $1,781 x 0.37 = $659 tax savings for business miles driven the first year.

Since the vehicle was driven 95% of the time for business, I was able to depreciate 95% of the cost of the vehicle, which came to $34,200. Multiplying that by my marginal tax rate of 37% gave me a $12,654 tax savings for depreciation.

I decided not to trade in my old car and instead sold it and carried the papers at 5% interest for five years. The price I collected for the car was $16,984 ($15,000 price + $1,984 interest).

So the total cost to me to trade my $15,000 car for a new $36,000 one was $1,091:

$$36,000 - 4,612 - 659 - 12,654 - 16,984 = \$1,091$$

Having my business buy the vehicle in this manner saved me $20,000 over the cost of buying the vehicle for personal use and trading in the old car. I also continued to get the mileage deduction each year.

COVER ANY TAX BURDEN BY WITHHOLDING FROM YOUR PROFESSIONAL OFFICE PAYROLL

This nice trick will help you avoid paying quarterly taxes on your real estate income. If your real estate business is creating a good profit that will lead to additional income taxes, then just make the adjustment on your regular job's payroll check—as long as your real estate business is being taxed under your Social Security number. This won't work if your business is a corporation, as the corporation may owe taxes separately from you.

If you think you will need to pay an extra $20,000 in federal taxes this year from your real estate profits and you get paid monthly at the office, increase your payroll tax withholding until it is an additional 1/12 of your expected taxes each month. In this case, an additional $1,667 per month in extra federal taxes would need to be withheld. You should account for your state taxes as well. If you get paid more frequently than once a month, then make the appropriate calculations so the entire $20,000 will have been paid by the end of the year.

You can either decrease your number of dependents/exemptions or you can just ask for an additional $1,667 to be taken out with each check for taxes, if you get paid monthly. As long as the IRS gets their money, they don't care how you give it to them. They will not be happy if you leave it all for April 15. They might impose a penalty to make up for their unhappiness.

PREPARING YOUR TAXES: KEEP GOOD RECORDS

Keeping good records is the key to getting your maximum tax write-offs. You do not want to pay more than your fair share of taxes. The IRS has rules and you need to follow them. But first you must know all the rules to play the game.

Here is where a good CPA comes in handy. But they can only work with the information you give them.

PASS-THROUGH ENTITY FOR TAKING PROFITS

Recently a new law was passed for pass-through business entities (as of this writing). Those are businesses that have their income pass through to the individual's personal income tax return like a real estate LLC would do. Your real estate should be taxed as a partnership, a pass-through LLC, or an S-corporation.

If your adjusted gross income is less than $315,000 and you are married and filing jointly, then you can usually take the deduction. You will get to write off 20% of your business taxable income and it will be written off separate from the standard deduction.

This is a very complicated new issue so please discuss this with your accountant so you can be sure you do everything right to get this valuable deduction. I was able to get this deduction by changing only one thing we were doing with our business in order to qualify. It is well worth looking into.

OTHER BUSINESS DEDUCTIONS

Many other things you will use in your life can be deducted by your real estate business. The key is you use them for the business and have the business purchase them.

Here are some great examples:

- Camera to photograph the properties before and after move-in
- Chainsaw to cut down tree limbs on properties
- Yard care tools to take care of the properties
- Computer to track income and expenses
- Phone to handle property business
- Internet to handle property business
- Utility trailer to haul off leftover junk
- Business travel to attend real estate conferences
- Business meetings with your business partner (spouse)
- Tools to repair things
- Shop vacuum for water cleanup
- Cleaning supplies
- Pressure washer
- Paint gun
- Backpack leaf blower
- Anything else you can use for the property, even though you sometimes "borrow" it to use at home

"Price is what you pay.
Value is what you get."

— Warren Buffett

Chapter 14

SELLING YOUR PROPERTY

As a real estate investor, selling your property usually isn't what you want to do. You should be buying good property you will hold for the rest of your life. That is the way you develop passive income. If you sell the property, you get a chunk of cash, have taxes to pay, and lose your cash flow. Then you will have to find a place to invest the money you received from the sale.

However, there may come a time when you do want to sell, like the situation that happened with the apartment I sold. We owned it in a partnership and it was time for the partnership to dissolve and move on. So the property needed to be sold. If something happens to you that leads you to sell a property, here is some information to help you.

CAPITAL GAINS

Selling your property outright is the most expensive option. In the last chapter, we talked about capital gains and ways to avoid them. If you sell your property, you will be dealing with those capital gains taxes. But there is a way to avoid them.

DO A 1031 EXCHANGE

The most important thing to remember is to do a 1031 exchange if you can. The 1031 exchange is a nice tax rule allowing you to defer capital gains on the appreciated value of your property upon its sale. You do this by "trading" your property for another property of like kind, of equal or greater value. Since you "trade" the property instead of selling it, you can sidestep the capital gains tax and kick that can down the road.

To qualify for a 1031 exchange, the property being traded must be of like kind. You can trade one apartment building for another, for instance. The new property must be of equal or greater value than the old property, so you are not putting any money in your pocket with the deal.

You will need an exchange facilitator who will be the go-between on the sale. When you sell your old property, the money will go to the facilitator and not to you. Then when you buy the new property, the money will come from the facilitator. You will pay a fee for the facilitator's services.

There are some strict time limits to follow when making this trade. From the time you close on the sale of your old property, you will have 45 days to declare the new property you plan to purchase. To be safe, you should declare more than one property, in case the sale of the one you wanted falls through. The other time constraint is you will have 180 days from the day the first property you sold closed escrow, to close escrow on the new property you are buying. There are some more details to each of those rules but you get the general idea. You can find the full details by looking up rule 1031 with the IRS.

If you trade to a property with less value than the one you sold, you will end up with some cash profit, called *boot*. You will have to pay capital gains taxes on the boot unless you can get that exchanged into an additional property. Avoid having any boot unless you really need some cash in your pocket.

TO BUY BIGGER PROPERTIES

Some investors use this rule to move up in property size when they otherwise could not afford to buy the bigger property at first. For example, they buy a $200,000 property with a $50,000 down payment. Five years later, the property is now worth $300,000 and the equity is about $150,000.

This property can be 1031 exchanged for a $600,000 property, using the $150,000 equity for the down payment on the next property. Five years later, the new property is worth about $750,000 and has $300,000 of equity. This is exchanged for a $1,000,000 property using the $300,000 equity as the down payment.

As you can see, you keep trading up, using the equity for a down payment on a more expensive property using the 1031 exchange. Originally you could not afford to put $300,000 down to buy the $1,000,000 property, but this way you have parlayed the $50,000 into a $1,000,000 property.

WHEN PROFIT EXCEEDS DEPRECIATION

Another technique used is to trade up when the profits on a property exceed the depreciation. This helps you to never pay taxes on your cash flow.

Suppose you hold the $1,000,000 property on a $150,000 piece of land. You could be depreciating $850,000. Depreciation is done over 27.5 years, so you get $30,909 of depreciation each year.

As the rents increase, eventually the taxable profit from the property will exceed this depreciation figure. When that happens, you can either start paying taxes on the portion of the cash flow profits that exceeds the depreciation—which will be small initially—or you can 1031 exchange to a bigger building and start again with a higher depreciation figure to shelter greater cash flow profits.

OTHER REASONS

There are other reasons to make a 1031 exchange, such as relocating to a new area and wanting your investment property to be near you. This is especially important if you are self-managing the property. If you retire and move to Arizona, you might want to exchange all your Chicago property for properties in Arizona.

If you want to have the cash from the sale and won't be doing an exchange, be sure to set aside the proper amount of money you will need to pay the capital gains taxes. Never spend the money you are supposed to use to pay taxes. That will get you into some real trouble with the IRS.

HOW TO SELL REAL ESTATE

When it comes time to sell, put in some effort to make your place more appealing, to get a good price or quicker offers. There are many things you can do such as paint the exterior, clean off the spider webs, plant flowers in the yard, trim all the bushes in the landscape, remove any dead trees, clean out the gutters, remove fallen leaves, and anything else you can see that doesn't look good when you stand on the curb and look at the property.

Take pictures of the inside of some of the best apartments. When you know you will be selling soon, take pictures of the next empty apartment when it is ready to rent. Take some nice pictures of the outside of the apartment when the trees are in bloom and pretty. These pictures will be used to advertise the sale and show prospective buyers what is there without needing to go inside.

Depending on your situation, you might or might not want to use a realtor or a real estate attorney to help you sell the property. If you are familiar enough with the process, you can save 6% of the sales price by selling the property yourself as a "for Sale by Owner." I have done several transactions this way and saved a lot of money. It is easy to do once you have experience buying and selling real estate. You might not want to try this the first time you sell a property. The first time, you can pay close attention to what the realtor actually does so you can do it yourself next time.

Prepare for the sale ahead of time. Have an accurate assessment of the value of the property and an accurate net operating income calculated to show potential buyers. Make copies of the last two tax returns and all the rental contracts. Make a simplified rent roll showing each apartment, its size, the tenant name and phone number, and the amount of rent they are paying. The new buyer will want this information. Be sure your presented numbers match the ones on your tax returns.

If you own the property without a mortgage and don't plan to do a 1031 exchange, consider carrying the loan for the next owner. This can be a great deal for you. I am carrying a loan currently on the property I sold. If they default, I will get the property back to sell again and I keep the down payment money, as well as any payments they have made up until that point. Great deal for me. If all goes well, I make interest at a decent rate for many years.

Collecting your monthly payments can also be automated. The title company will draw up the loan agreement during escrow. Be sure you read it to confirm it is correct. You can have a loan servicing company collect the payments and keep track of the amount of interest and principal you are receiving. For the loan I'm carrying now, the buyer and the seller are each charged $6 a month for this service. The buyer sends each monthly check to the loan servicing center and they record it and electronically deposit the money into my bank account, minus the $6 fee. Even when I am away on vacation, the money is getting put into my account. If the buyer is late, the loan servicing company collects the late fees. When the loan is paid off, they will take care of transferring the title to the buyer as free and clear of all mortgages. If the buyer stops making payments and I start the repossession process, there is a third party to certify that the payments are not being made.

Carrying the loan when you sell a property has some great tax advantages. The interest you earn will be taxed as earned income in the year you receive it. A big benefit of carrying the mortgage is in delaying the capital gains taxes on the sale of the property. When you hold the mortgage, you didn't get paid your capital gains yet so you don't yet owe the taxes. Every year some of the capital gains will be paid and then you will owe the taxes. This has the effect of spreading your capital gains out over the life of the loan.

Seller carry also makes the property more appealing to the new buyer. I mentioned earlier about all the advantages that seller financing brings to the buyer. Those advantages will now make your property more appealing to potential buyers than properties that will need to get conventional financing.

ROLE OF THE REALTOR

Many people are reluctant to sell property without a realtor. It is not as scary as it seems. In reality, the realtor is not doing a lot for you when it comes to selling commercial property such as apartments, and they collect a huge fee for their effort. They can do a lot for you when you are the buyer as you get them to do the legwork of finding good properties and then the seller will pay them their fee. Now you are the seller and you do not need to pay that fee.

The realtor will list your property for sale. You can do that by putting it in the paper, on Craigslist, and putting a sign out in front of the building. There are not many apartment buildings for sale. If you are selling a single-family home, having the realtor place your property in the MLS (Multiple Listings

Service) listing so all the other realtors can see it helps you be found. But investors who are looking for apartments will find you anyway. There is not a lot of noise to cut through.

When it comes to showing the place to prospective buyers, that doesn't happen with apartments like it does with houses. If you put a house for sale, many people might want to walk through it. It would be a burden on you to have to be there for all those walk-throughs. In that case, you might be money ahead to use a realtor.

Apartments don't have a walk-through until they are in escrow. So, in general, it will only happen once. Buyers will drive by and look at it and ask for pictures and ask for financials. Showing an apartment complex is not the same time burden as showing a house.

The buyer's realtor writes up the offer and presents it. If the buyer doesn't know how, you can write up their offer for them by downloading a form, or by getting a form for selling real estate from a stationary store. It doesn't matter who writes up the offer, it only matters that you both agree on it. Another option is to have the offer written up by a real estate attorney. They tend to charge less than a realtor.

The realtor gets in the middle of any negotiations and may play a good role in helping you make decisions about an offer. Few realtors are really good at this. If you know of one who is, then that may be a good reason to pay a realtor. Especially if you feel your negotiating skills are weak.

Once the offer is agreed on, the paperwork is sent to the escrow agent. They do all the real heavy lifting of the sale. They draw up all the paperwork and contracts for the sale and record the sale with the county. The realtor has nothing to do with this process.

If you have a property management company, they can get involved in having the apartment shown after the offer is accepted and getting access to the property for any needed inspections.

If you would like to do the work the realtor does, which is not a lot, you will be able to save a big chunk of money in the process. If you do not live where the property is located, you will need the help of a realtor for sure.

Chapter 15

GET STARTED . . . YOU WON'T REGRET IT

Now you are ready to get started. With every big new adventure, there's a risk you will fall into analysis paralysis and not take the first step. I don't want you to get stuck. It's time to go into action and become a real estate investor.

You do not need all your ducks in a row before you make your first offer. Remember, it will take several weeks to close on an offer. So if you don't have your LLC set up yet, it is no big deal. You will have it ready by the time the deal closes. If you don't, then you can transfer the property ownership to the LLC when it is complete.

You can do it. If my grandparents, who quit school after the eighth grade, could do this, then you certainly can. Every day someone is buying another investment property, and it's time that someone was you.

Get started on this list today and before you know it, you will be a real estate investor too. Then you are only a hop, skip, and a jump away from financial independence. Once you get started, read this book again. Every time you evaluate a property, read the pertinent chapter again. If you are the manager, read the management chapter every year. Subscribe to my blog at DrCorySFawcett.com and get involved in any groups I set up that will pertain to you, such as Facebook, Twitter, and others. And if you need any coaching, I'll be available to hire to help you along the way.

TEN STEPS TO BECOMING A REAL ESTATE INVESTOR

I have 10 steps for you to use in getting started today. You don't have to do them in order and you don't have to finish one step before moving onto the next. Several of the steps can be done simultaneously. The goal is to make an offer on a property within 90 days from now.

I know that sounds like a tall order, but you can do this. You are already a busy professional so you know how to get things done. You just need to make this a priority and get this done *now*. It will be a lot easier than you think and probably a lot easier than whatever you are currently doing in the business world. The first real estate investment you buy will be the hardest and scariest. They get easier after that, so get that first one out of the way now.

Here's what you should do next:

1. LEARN THE REAL ESTATE GAME

If I have convinced you that you can do this, then don't make this the only real estate book you read. Many books are available. Look for other books that will help you find, evaluate, and manage real estate, and start reading them.

Because there are so many different niches in real estate investing, I don't want to make any book recommendations here. You decide first on the type of investing you want to do and find books that talk about that niche. If you want to own mini storage units, it will do you no good to read the best book in the world about flipping single-family homes. You don't have time to read books about things you don't want to do.

Look for blogs, podcasts, newsletters, and forums on real estate investing in your chosen sector. In the beginning, spend at least 30 minutes each day on your real estate continuing education. The more you know, the more comfortable you will be in all aspects of real estate investing.

Get a copy of the game *Cash Flow*, created by Robert Kiyosaki, the author of *Rich Dad Poor Dad*. This game is similar to Monopoly but much more realistic in teaching you what it is like to develop a positive cash flow using real estate. Play it with your kids and they will learn these lessons as well. We began playing Cash Flow with our kids in their early teens and they really enjoyed it. They learned lessons that they are applying today.

2. FIND A REALTOR

Begin looking for a realtor. Ask other real estate investors who they are using. Interview some of their recommendations. You are looking for a realtor who has done some real estate investing themselves. You need someone who will not pester you with places to see that do not meet your criteria. You are too busy to look at lots of property. You need only examine the "plums."

List the criteria you will use to screen property. This will be what you want your realtor to look for. If you give them a target, they can hit it. You can start with the list I gave you earlier in the book and modify it to meet your needs.

3. EXAMINE YOUR MARKET

Drive the neighborhoods and check out what is right under your nose. You will be surprised at what you find. Now you are looking at the town through the eyes of a real estate investor and it will look different.

Every day, take a different route to and from work. This will give you a good perspective without taking much time. Keep your eyes open. Look for small apartment complexes that you never noticed before. Look at the cars in the neighborhood. Think about how easy the neighborhood will be to access from your home or work location.

Look in the newspaper in the "property for sale" section. Look on Craigslist and Zillow. Watch for those "for sale" signs in the yards, especially those that say for sale by owner. Within one month of beginning to examine your local market, you will have gained a vast new knowledge that will help you move forward.

4. DEFINE YOUR NICHE

Don't try to be everything to everyone. As a general surgeon, I had a niche. I did not do orthopedics or treat heart attacks. I had one area and I learned everything about that one area. Treat your real estate business the same.

Figure out what type of investment you would be comfortable with. Is it single-family homes, small apartments, big apartments, commercial, partnerships, or medical office buildings? There are many niches in real estate and you need to start with one of them. You can branch out to others later.

5. FIND A BANKER

Most deals are done with conventional financing. Most people are familiar with that. So there is a high likelihood that you will do a conventional deal and need a bank to be involved. Go to several banks in the area. Look at national banks, regional banks, local banks, and credit unions.

When I first started, I found one person I liked who managed a bank and I went back to him every time. I liked the way he worked, and he got to know me. When they know you and have confidence in what you are doing, they are much more likely to give you a loan and with better terms.

Find one or two you really like and keep going back to them. But keep other avenues open as well. Sometimes one bank will not do a deal that another will.

6. MEET PROPERTY MANAGEMENT TEAMS

Interview a few property management companies. Start with the ones other real estate investors use and recommend. You will likely need some help from them, even if you are managing the property yourself. I used them for evictions early on. Later, when I began to travel, I turned everything over to one company.

You will get a good vibe from some and not feel comfortable with others. Find one that would like to work with you and you will have a great tool in your back pocket.

7. FORM YOUR LLC AND FIND YOUR PROFESSIONALS

It is not crucial that you have an LLC for your investment real estate, but as a professional, I would recommend it. It keeps your real estate business clearly separated from everything else you do. It also provides you a level of protection against lawsuits that might come up.

You do not need to do this to become an investor. You do not need it completed before you buy your first property. But you can start the ball rolling.

Find an attorney and a CPA you like and who are good with real estate businesses. They all have niches too.

Interview contractors whom you will occasionally need for bigger projects. I once replaced all the decks and railings at two of my apartments and hired a contractor to do the job. Pick out a paint store, floor covering store, appliance store, an electrician, and a plumber who you will use. Get to know them and open an account for your real estate business.

8. MAKE AN OFFER

If you stumble onto a property right away that looks good to you, go for it. Do not wait until you have all your ducks in a row. You will greatly speed up the learning process by having a property in escrow.

You will never get anywhere without making some offers. Don't be afraid to make the offer. They might say no, they might counteroffer, or they might say yes. No matter what happens, you will have made your first offer and that first offer is the toughest one. It is the one thing keeping most people from becoming real estate investors; they never make an offer.

That first offer was scary for me. After I had done it once, the rest were easy. The realtor and the escrow agent will walk you through the process. You don't actually need to know anything for this step because they know what to do.

Be sure you have accurately determined the cash flow of the property and that your offer will be viable as an investment. Evaluating a property is the most important step in the entire process. After all, you are doing this to create long-term passive income that will take care of you and your family for the rest of their lives. Make sure you will make money with every offer.

9. CLOSE ON YOUR FIRST PROPERTY

Someone will say yes to your offer to buy their property. Then you will set in motion an automated process in escrow, complete your due diligence inspections, and you will soon be signing the papers that will make you a real estate investor.

During the time you are in escrow, you will be able to set up the systems and teams you will need for the smooth running of the property. You can contact the people you will need to assemble your team. The first property you buy is the hardest and the one that will be the most time consuming. The second property will drop into an already running and oiled machine.

I only had to go to medical school once. You will only have to set up the system once.

10. CELEBRATE THE FACT THAT YOU ARE A REAL ESTATE INVESTOR

Celebrating your wins is something busy professionals don't tend to do. Time is a precious commodity and we don't like wasting it. Many of us consider celebrating a waste of time. In my opinion, you need to rethink this concept.

You have just accomplished something many only dream about. Take a moment to pat yourself on the back and relish in the accomplishment. Life should not be all work and no play. Put in some play with a purpose and celebrate the big wins in your life.

GO FOR IT

There you have it. I hope you realize now that real estate investing is not so hard, not so risky, and not so scary—it is something even a busy professional can do. Great wealth is built through real estate investing and it's time you put some of that wealth into your pocket.

I did this as a full-time general surgeon, so I know it can be done. I also know it can be done with very little time out of your busy schedule. It is not too difficult, but it will require some effort. Success is not given out freely—you have to earn it.

You are not too old to get started, no matter how old you are. Yes, it would have been better if you started earlier. Five years from now you don't want to say, "I wish I had started earlier." Today is tomorrow's earlier, so start today. If you have read this far, you have what it takes to become a real estate investor.

So what are you waiting for? Get out there and start investing. Your success is my goal and you will never succeed until you start. If you don't step out of your comfort zone, nothing will change.

"He is not a full man who does not own a piece of land."

— Hebrew proverb

"Every person who invests in well-selected real estate in a growing section of a prosperous community adopts the surest and safest method of becoming independent, for real estate is the basis of wealth."

— Theodore Roosevelt

ACKNOWLEDGMENTS

Many people contributed to the knowledge contained in this book, but I need to give a special thanks to my grandparents, Orshal and Virginia Brown, who introduced me to the concept of real estate investing. I need to thank my wife, Carolyn, who convinced me we had enough real estate to take care of our financial needs for the rest of our lives. She got me to stop buying more and start living more. Thanks to my father, Jim Fawcett, who was reluctant to become the maintenance man for my properties and yet was soon teaching me how to fix stuff. My kids Brian and Keith were around to help when I needed an extra hand. And thanks to Grants Pass Property Management, who have been taking care of my properties since I retired from my medical practice. They allow me to travel the world. I am ever thankful for my CPA, Ken Beheymer, for his needed and timely advice, and my attorney, Ben Feudenburg, whom I reach out to from time to time with legal questions.

A special thanks to those who did the test reading of this book and offered suggested improvements: Allison Batchelor, M.D.; Pastor Bob Bonner; J. Brant Darby, DDS; Haitham Haddad, M.D.; Jim Lafeber; Dan Lane; Hernan Lopez-Morra, M.D.; Jeffrey G. Wiencek, M.D.; my son Brian Fawcett; and my lovely wife, Carolyn Fawcett.

There are many others along the way who contributed to the information I've learned through the years and am now passing on to you. I'm sorry I can't list them all, or even remember them all, as they are too numerous to count.

I am ever thankful for those who continue to buy and read the books in the *Doctors Guide* series. You make me want to write more. Thanks for your support.

Thanks to the team at Aloha Publishing, including Maryanna Young and Jennifer Regner, and the Fusion Creative Works design team of Shiloh Schroeder, Rachel Langaker, and Jessi Carpenter. Without them, this book would still be just an idea floating around in my mind.

ABOUT THE AUTHOR

Dr. Cory S. Fawcett's passion for teaching personal finance spans his entire career. Through one-on-one counseling, as a Crown Financial Ministries small group discussion leader (a 10-week Bible study on money management), and as a keynote speaker, he has been improving people's financial and professional lives for years. As an instructor for medical students and residents, he has found they have a hunger and need for financial wisdom and direction as they transform into practicing physicians. He is the author of *The Doctors Guide* book series, all of which have become award-winning and best-selling, including *The Doctors Guide to Starting Your Practice/Career Right, The Doctors Guide to Eliminating Debt,* and *The Doctors Guide to Smart Career Alternatives and Retirement.*

With his financial interest and background knowledge, he has served on several boards and financial committees throughout the years. He has been involved as owner, founder, or partner in more than two dozen business and real estate ventures.

His current mission is teaching doctors to have healthy, happy, and debt-free lives—to regain control of their practice, their time, and their finances. He is writing, speaking, and coaching in an effort to improve the lives of his colleagues. Burnout, suicide, debt, and bankruptcy are increasing among physicians, dentists, optometrists, chiropractors, pharmacists, nurse practitioners, and others in the healthcare industry, and he focuses on halting the progression of these unnecessary outcomes.

Dr. Fawcett is an award-winning and best-selling author, keynote speaker, entrepreneur, and a repurposed general surgeon. He completed his bachelor's degree in biology at Stanford University, his Doctor of Medicine at Oregon Health Sciences University, and his general surgery residency at Kern Medical Center. After completing his training, he returned to southern Oregon to practice for 20 years in a single-specialty private practice group in Grants Pass. Then for three years, he worked part time in rural hospitals providing call coverage before devoting his time to helping healthcare professionals thrive.

Since 1988, he has shared his home with his lovely bride, Carolyn. They have two boys: Brian, who graduated from college with a degree in economics, and Keith, who graduated with a degree in mobile development.

ABOUT *THE DOCTORS GUIDE* SERIES

The Doctors Guide series aims to improve the lives of doctors on both a personal and a financial level and includes the following:

The Doctors Guide to Starting Your Practice/Career Right

Every resident should read this book as they start their final year of training. I wish it would be given out in every residency program. If that would happen, the state of medicine in America would be greatly improved.

This is the book that will help the resident doctor make a smooth and successful transition into the life of an attending. Whether as a business owner or an employed physician, there are so many things to consider. This book will pave the way to success.

The Doctors Guide to Eliminating Debt

Debt has become a terrible burden for many of my colleagues. It's not just the debt they accumulate during their training. Once that attending income begins to roll in, everyone wants to lend the new doctor some money. The tendency to take those loans has put many a doctor into financial bondage.

It is time we all stop managing our debt and start eliminating it. We must work hard to eliminate Debtabetic Neuropathy and Alzheimer's Debtmentia in our lifetime. Lifelong debt is not the best path.

The Doctors Guide to Smart Career Alternatives and Retirement

Many physicians are hurting today and feel betrayed by their profession. They are ready to leave medicine after all those years to get here. There are alternatives to this path. This book walks you through three options: Changes you can make to enjoy your practice more, new career alternatives for physicians that build on your vast knowledge, and if neither of those will work, then it becomes a how-to guide to wind down a practice and retire.

The Doctors Guide to Real Estate Investing for Busy Professionals

Many busy professionals think they don't have enough time to invest in real estate. They have the mistaken notion that it takes more time than they have. When other physicians found out I managed 64 apartment units, they were always surprised. "How can you possibly have time for that?" was the most common question. In this book, I show you exactly how you can have time to invest in real estate even if you are a busy professional.

The Doctors Guide to Thriving in Locum Tenens

This is an online video course for everything you need to know to get involved in locum tenens. Many doctors are thinking about it but are not sure what to do. I spent three years doing locum tenens and put all the information I learned into this course so you don't have to reinvent the wheel. Whether you want to do locums full time, part time, or just one weekend a month, this course will help you be successful.

QUESTIONS? COMMENTS?

Dr. Cory S. Fawcett
FinancialSuccessMD.com

I wrote this book to share what I have learned as a real estate investor. It certainly is possible for busy professionals to buy and manage investment real estate, and that includes you. I also want to hear about your experiences. Any feedback is welcome, and I want to know if you think I've missed an important topic, you have a story to tell, or you found a mistake. Also, I didn't put everything I know into this book. Send me an email at md@financialsuccessmd.com or contact me through my website at FinancialSuccessMD.com.

If you found this book to be useful, please post a review on Amazon, spread the word in social media, and pass on what you have learned to your colleagues.

Connect with Financial Success MD on LinkedIn
Like @FinancialSuccessMD on Facebook
Follow @Fin_SuccessMD on Twitter
Email md@financialsuccessmd.com
Watch Financial Success MD on YouTube
Follow my blog at FinancialSuccessMD.com
Join me at financialsuccessmd on Instagram
Pin me at financialsuccessmd on Pinterest

Made in the USA
Las Vegas, NV
07 July 2021